The Crass Menagerie

Other *Pearls Before Swine* Collections

The Sopratos

Da Brudderhood of Zeeba Zeeba Eata

The Ratvolution Will Not Be Televised

Nighthogs

This Little Piggy Stayed Home

BLTs Taste So Darn Good

Treasuries

Lions and Tigers and Crocs, Oh My!

Sgt. Piggy's Lonely Hearts Club Comic

The Crass Menagerie

A *Pearls Before Swine* Treasury

by Stephan Pastis

Andrews McMeel
Publishing, LLC

Kansas City

Pearls Before Swine is distributed internationally by United Feature Syndicate.

The Crass Menagerie copyright © 2008 by Stephan Pastis. All rights reserved. Printed in the United States of America. No part of this book may be used or reproduced in any manner whatsoever without written permission except in the case of reprints in the context of reviews. For information, write Andrews McMeel Publishing, LLC, an Andrews McMeel Universal company, 4520 Main Street, Kansas City, Missouri 64111.

08 09 10 11 12 BAM 10 9 8 7 6 5 4 3 2 1

ISBN-13: 978-0-7407-7100-2
ISBN-10: 0-7407-7100-0

Library of Congress Control Number: 2007937785

www.andrewsmcmeel.com

Pearls Before Swine can be viewed on the Internet at
www.comics.com/comics/pearls.

These strips appeared in newspapers from January 24, 2005, to August 6, 2006.

INTRODUCTION

It started out like any other drive in my mom's gold Buick.

I was five years old and we had just dropped off my grandmother at my other grandmother's house in San Gabriel, California.

My mom drove. My older sister Parisa sat in the front seat. And I sat alone in the back.

As we watched my grandmother walk toward the house and wave goodbye, my mom backed out of the driveway and began driving down the street. And I, with that feeling of safety and security that can only come with being a five-year-old boy in the backseat of his parents' car, leaned snugly against the car door my grandmother had just shut.

Safe. Secure.

And that's when the car door popped open.

Out I fell, hitting the pavement with a thud. I rolled and rolled, finally coming to rest against the side of the curb.

And that wasn't the worst part.

The worst part was looking up and seeing my mom's car still driving away.

Talk about a life-changing event.

So there I was. Five years old and lying in some random gutter. Not a lot of options for getting home when you're five years old and lying in some random gutter. But it did give me time to think. And think I did. And foremost on my five-year-old mind was this:

"Why'd my mom just put a hit on me?"

I knew I had been an unruly kid. I never stopped talking. I never listened. And I couldn't seem to perform my one and only chore, that of emptying all the little trash-cans in the house into the large metal trashcan outside. It seemed beneath me.

But a hit? That seemed like an overreaction.

I knew also that I had been a demanding kid. When my mom wouldn't let me have my way, I used to bang my head into the kitchen floor until she relented. And this was no ordinary head-banging. This was a convincing, no-holds-barred, concussions-don't-faze-me head-banging. So naturally, I prevailed.

And when she wanted to punish me, she couldn't, because she couldn't catch me. With the speed and grace of a gazelle, I would run behind a large three-piece sectional couch we had in the den. She'd try to chase me, but after a few laps around this gigantic couch, she'd be out of gas. The wise move would have been for her to just climb over the center of the couch and grab me, but this was Mom. And agility was not her forte.

But she was not without options. Early on, she learned a trick that had a devastating impact on my little psyche.

She'd pick up the phone to call our priest.

Why it was that her calling the priest worried me so, I know not. But it did. And it always brought me running out from behind that big couch and straight into the kitch-en, where I'd tug on my mom's arm and beg her to stop dialing the numbers.

But even this trick eventually lost its effectiveness. That occurred when I noticed she was dialing a different number every time she called the priest. Now either that priest was changing his phone number every week or my mom was faking the whole thing. When I finally realized it was the latter, the jig was up.

And so the hit.

It was not a skilled hit. Nor artful. But it was a hit. And she had not acted alone.

First, there was my grandmother, whose job it was to leave the car door partially ajar when she closed it. This was the most skilled act in the entire operation. It's not easy to pretend to close a car door while not really closing it.

Then there was my other grandmother, the one whose house we were traveling to. I'm not sure what her job was. I guess it was to just stand on the porch and wave, thereby distracting me so I would not notice the car door partially left open by the other grandmother. Not a terribly important role, but probably still worth some of the hit money.

But as any faithful *Sopranos* fan knows, few hits go off as cleanly as planned. And this was no exception. Because this gang of assassins had failed to plan for one contingency:

Parisa.

You see, no one had let my older sister in on the plan. Perhaps they had not expected her to be sitting in the front seat. Perhaps they had simply taken her support for granted. Whatever the explanation, the fact remained: She had not gotten the memo.

So when her brother went flying out the back door of the car, she hopped out too. She ran toward me crying, "Stephan, my Stephan" and scooped me out of the gutter.

I never saw the look on the faces of my mother and grandmothers as Parisa carried me back toward the car, but it had to be one of disappointment. They had not only bungled a simple operation; they had ensured I would now be unbearably cocky.

But that was then. And this is now. And the subject of the assassination attempt rarely comes up at Christmas dinner. It is one of those family differences that we've simply chosen to set aside.

In the few times the topic has been raised during the last thirty or so years, my mother has denied any wrongdoing, stating simply, "You idiot. The door just wasn't closed tightly enough."

No one believes her.

But that is of no matter now. The fact is that I am here. And so is my sister, without whom Rat, Pig, Goat, Zebra, and the Brudderhood of Zeeba Zeeba Eata crocodiles would not exist. Today she lives in Rocklin, California, and only occasionally regrets her actions that day.

So if you like the strip, and come upon her while walking along the streets of Rocklin one day, please give her your thanks. And if you don't like the strip. . . well . . . know that it's all her fault.

But in either case, be careful of an angry, older woman in a large gold Buick.

She can be trouble.

Stephan Pastis
March 2008

For my Mom, hit or no hit

Whenever I have Rat or Pig writing on a computer, the monitor I draw is from an old Apple IIC computer, which came out almost twenty-five years ago. One would think they would have upgraded by now, but one would be wrong.

This was a very popular strip. I think Pig's sweetness really helps balance out the strip.

This was a classic case of regionalism affecting my strip. In California, we have something called a "Denver omelet," which is an omelet filled with ham, bell peppers, and onions. But other parts of the country know it as a "Western omelet," and still other parts of the country don't know what either omelet is. As a result, this strip confused about two-thirds of the country. It happens.

After making fun of *Cathy* relentlessly, I thought it was only fair to have her character ripping on me for a change.

Drawing bowling pins is very hard if your name is Stephan Pastis. Thus, this will be my first and last series set in a bowling alley.

This one involved drawing both bowling pins *and* trash cans. Wow. Sometimes I go all out.

I like the bowling pin's speech in the second panel. It's pretty much how I look at life.

Pig's comments in the second panel are taken from the speech Richard Nixon gave to his White House staff on the day he resigned the presidency.

I was surprised some people didn't get this. The message being held up by the pigs is "Go mate," as in "Go do the thing that leads to having babies."

I hate eating in fancy restaurants, mostly because I feel so bad for the waiter who has to keep filling my water glass. It makes me not want to drink any water.

A good example of the contrast between Rat and Pig.

Originally, I had Rat swearing in the second panel here, but then I thought it was a little too much given that he had just sworn at the customer in the Monday strip (2/7). Thus, I got rid of the word.

17

This was a very popular strip among waiters and waitresses.

By this time, Rat had gone four days without swearing. Thus, it was time to have Rat swear again.

After this ran, I heard from food editors at two different *Times Union* newspapers that *Pearls* runs in. They were great sports about the strip.

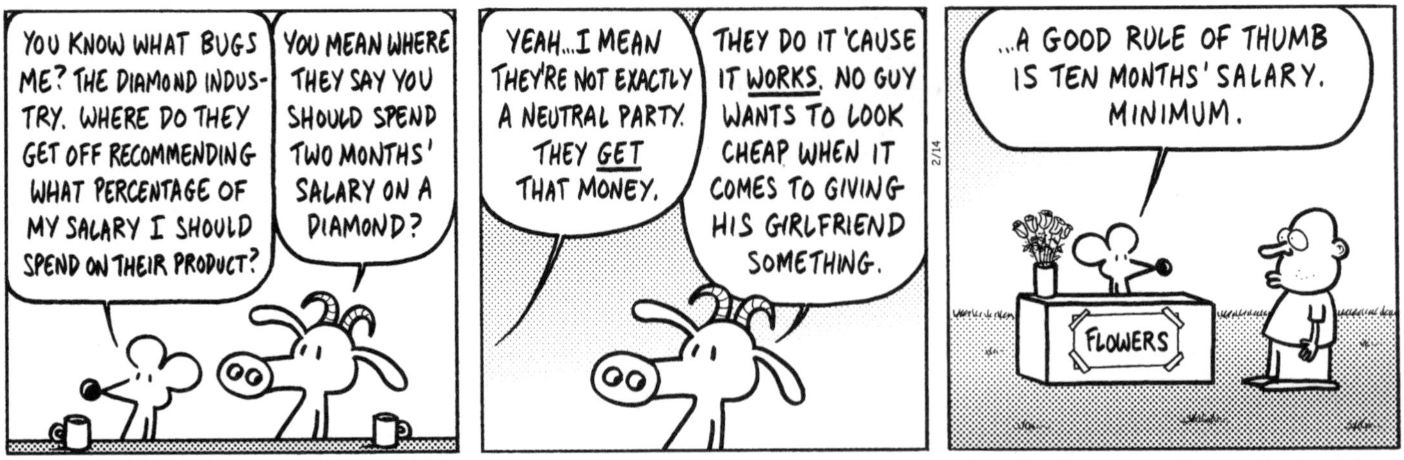
YOU KNOW WHAT BUGS ME? THE DIAMOND INDUSTRY. WHERE DO THEY GET OFF RECOMMENDING WHAT PERCENTAGE OF MY SALARY I SHOULD SPEND ON THEIR PRODUCT?
YOU MEAN WHERE THEY SAY YOU SHOULD SPEND TWO MONTHS' SALARY ON A DIAMOND?
YEAH...I MEAN THEY'RE NOT EXACTLY A NEUTRAL PARTY. THEY GET THAT MONEY.
THEY DO IT 'CAUSE IT WORKS. NO GUY WANTS TO LOOK CHEAP WHEN IT COMES TO GIVING HIS GIRLFRIEND SOMETHING.
2/14
...A GOOD RULE OF THUMB IS TEN MONTHS' SALARY. MINIMUM.
FLOWERS

Judging by how much a dozen roses costs around Valentine's Day, it appears that the flower industry is already following this rule.

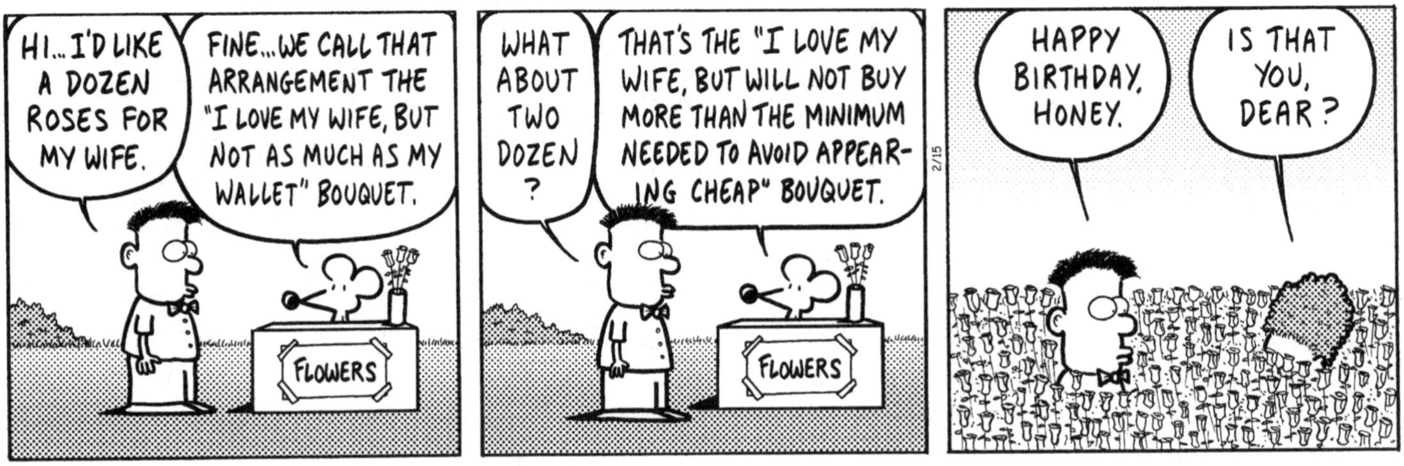
HI...I'D LIKE A DOZEN ROSES FOR MY WIFE.
FINE...WE CALL THAT ARRANGEMENT THE "I LOVE MY WIFE, BUT NOT AS MUCH AS MY WALLET" BOUQUET.
FLOWERS
WHAT ABOUT TWO DOZEN?
THAT'S THE "I LOVE MY WIFE, BUT WILL NOT BUY MORE THAN THE MINIMUM NEEDED TO AVOID APPEARING CHEAP" BOUQUET.
FLOWERS
2/15
HAPPY BIRTHDAY, HONEY.
IS THAT YOU, DEAR?

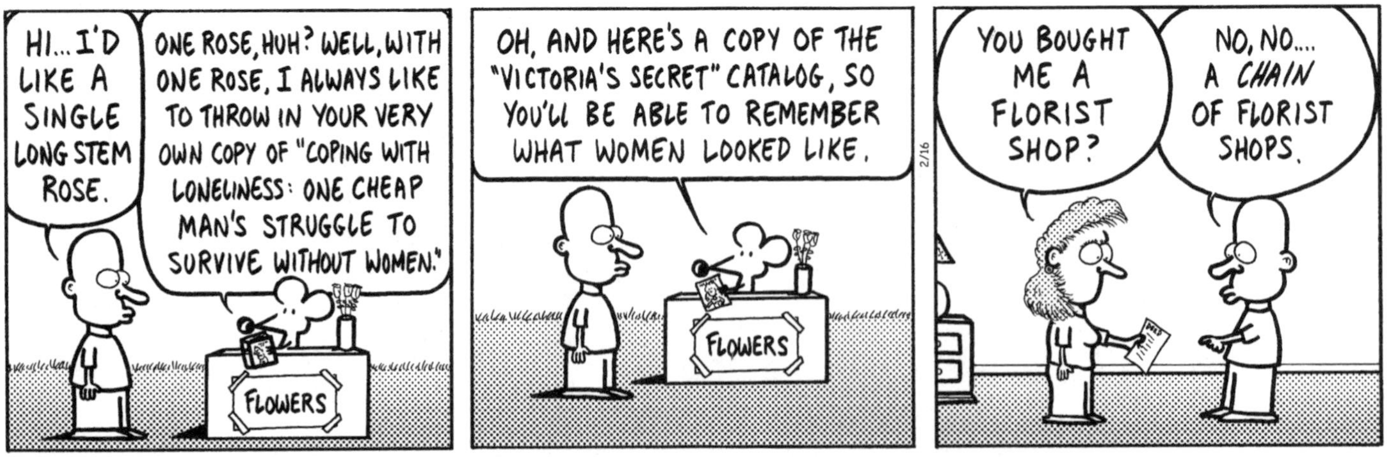
HI...I'D LIKE A SINGLE LONG STEM ROSE.
ONE ROSE, HUH? WELL, WITH ONE ROSE, I ALWAYS LIKE TO THROW IN YOUR VERY OWN COPY OF "COPING WITH LONELINESS: ONE CHEAP MAN'S STRUGGLE TO SURVIVE WITHOUT WOMEN."
FLOWERS
OH, AND HERE'S A COPY OF THE "VICTORIA'S SECRET" CATALOG, SO YOU'LL BE ABLE TO REMEMBER WHAT WOMEN LOOKED LIKE.
FLOWERS
2/16
YOU BOUGHT ME A FLORIST SHOP?
NO, NO.... A CHAIN OF FLORIST SHOPS.

That's one heck of an elongated forehead on that fellow. Not sure what I was going for that day.

I thought I'd hear from angry *Star Trek* fans about this one, but I didn't. Apparently, they have conceded the fact that they have trouble attracting women.

This one might win you some bar bets with other *Pearls* readers. Ask someone, "Has Pig ever killed anyone in the strip?" The answer is yes.

I've never put chains on a car in my life. I've never even seen someone else putting chains on a car. In fact, I've never seen snow fall. I feel oddly unqualified to have drawn this strip.

I believe this was the first time the crocs appeared in a Sunday strip. It's funny for me to look back and see how differently I first drew them. For example, if you look at current strips, you'll see that the humps on their head are now much more pronounced and their snouts are much narrower.

In the original of this strip, the line in the last panel was, "I wouldn't recommend that," meaning that Pig shouldn't try to shake hands with a guy who has none. But it made it look like he was being warned that the torso-less guy was going to try to shake Pig's hand with some *other* part of his body (a part I can't mention in polite company), and thus the strip looked too inappropriate, even for me. Thus, I deleted that line and I changed it to the punchline you see here. The original of this strip can be seen in the "Not Ready for Prime Time Comic Strips" section of this book.

The crocs talked a little differently early on. For example, I used to drop all the "R"s ("vewy," "favoweet," "hungwee"). Other than with the word "zeeba," I don't think I do that anymore.

The fact that everyone, even the guy's brother, would take advantage of a guy with no upper torso makes me laugh. I'm not sure what that says about me.

More dropped "R"s. It looks so odd to me now.

If I had to do it over, I'd lay out this week of strips differently. I had two different sets of strips, the half-brother ones and the croc ones, and I interspersed them so that each series ran every other day. I think now that that was a little disorienting. I should have run the three half-brother strips consecutively. I think I did it at the time so that readers wouldn't get bored of seeing the same story line for three consecutive days.

Every guy's dream (minus the choking and dying part).

Every now and then, I like to throw in a series where Pig is vulnerable. It helps to balance out the tone of the strip. More importantly, I draw a wonderful oven mitt.

I had to borrow a spatula from the kitchen to know how to draw this one. But I must say, between the spatula and the oven mitt, I've got the drawing of kitchen items down *cold*.

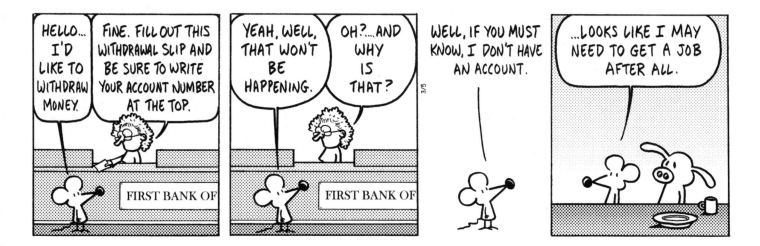

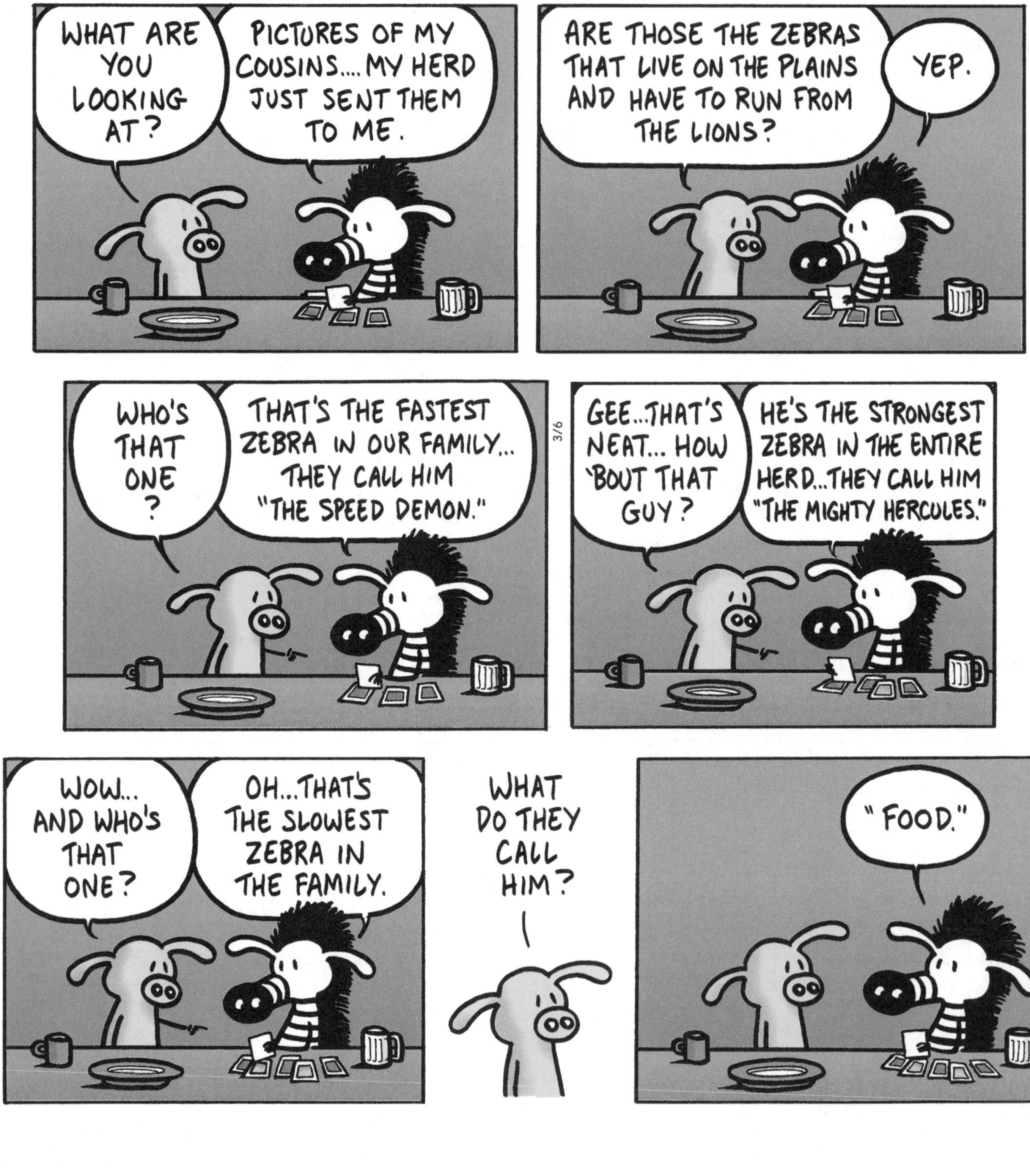
WHAT ARE YOU LOOKING AT?
PICTURES OF MY COUSINS.... MY HERD JUST SENT THEM TO ME.
ARE THOSE THE ZEBRAS THAT LIVE ON THE PLAINS AND HAVE TO RUN FROM THE LIONS?
YEP.
WHO'S THAT ONE ?
THAT'S THE FASTEST ZEBRA IN OUR FAMILY... THEY CALL HIM "THE SPEED DEMON."
GEE...THAT'S NEAT... HOW 'BOUT THAT GUY?
HE'S THE STRONGEST ZEBRA IN THE ENTIRE HERD...THEY CALL HIM "THE MIGHTY HERCULES."
WOW... AND WHO'S THAT ONE?
OH...THAT'S THE SLOWEST ZEBRA IN THE FAMILY.
WHAT DO THEY CALL HIM?
"FOOD."

It has always astounded me that people will pay money to have a star named after them. To me, it is no different than having a grain of sand named after you.

My view of humanity in a nutshell.

Ah. Social commentary. Move over, *Doonesbury*.

Wow. This one's pretty surreal. More importantly, I spent way too much time drawing that window in the first panel.

I very rarely see something and then draw it straight into the strip. But I did with this one. One morning, I happened to go to a very large and well-known store just after it opened, and I saw all the employees being made to yell a cheer. I can't explain why, but it really depressed me. It just seemed so demeaning and unnecessary. So I came home and drew this Sunday strip.

This strip marked the introduction of the Guard Duck, a character that turned out to be much more popular than I thought he'd be. Thus, he became a regular. I now see him as the sixth major character in the strip (after Rat, Pig, Goat, Zebra, and the crocs).

32

I really loved this strip, but it didn't seem to get a big reaction. It reminds me of the old *Saturday Night Live* skits where the Land Shark would knock on potential victims' front doors and lie about who he was.

It took me forever to find a Shakespeare quote that I could apply to the crocs.

This was a really popular strip. I think part of the reason the crocs work humor-wise is how quickly they turn on each other.

I took my family to Disneyland last year and there was one ride (having something to do with *Toy Story*, I think) where you had a little laser gun and could shoot stuff as you traveled through the ride. I think they should add that feature to "It's a Small World."

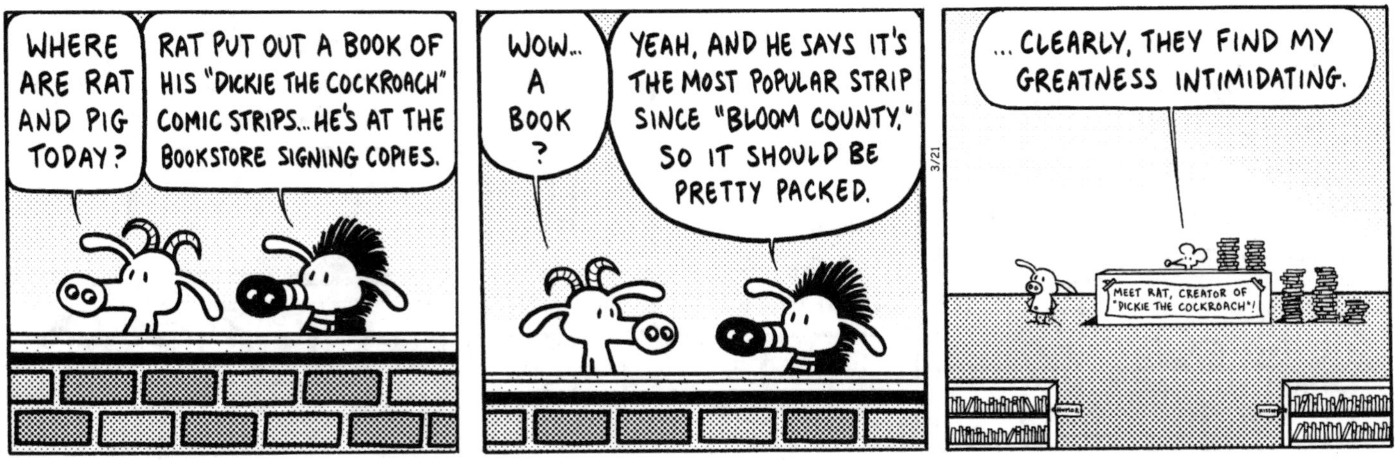
WHERE ARE RAT AND PIG TODAY?
RAT PUT OUT A BOOK OF HIS "DICKIE THE COCKROACH" COMIC STRIPS... HE'S AT THE BOOKSTORE SIGNING COPIES.
WOW... A BOOK?
YEAH, AND HE SAYS IT'S THE MOST POPULAR STRIP SINCE "BLOOM COUNTY." SO IT SHOULD BE PRETTY PACKED.
3/21
... CLEARLY, THEY FIND MY GREATNESS INTIMIDATING.
MEET RAT, CREATOR OF "DICKIE THE COCKROACH"!

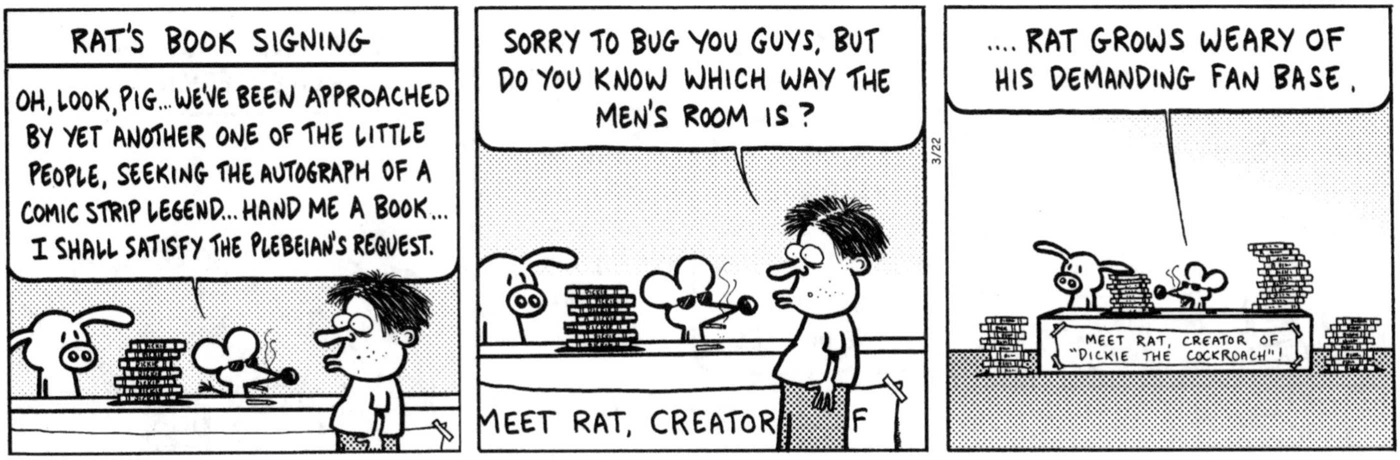
RAT'S BOOK SIGNING
OH, LOOK, PIG... WE'VE BEEN APPROACHED BY YET ANOTHER ONE OF THE LITTLE PEOPLE, SEEKING THE AUTOGRAPH OF A COMIC STRIP LEGEND... HAND ME A BOOK... I SHALL SATISFY THE PLEBEIAN'S REQUEST.
SORRY TO BUG YOU GUYS, BUT DO YOU KNOW WHICH WAY THE MEN'S ROOM IS?
MEET RAT, CREATOR F
3/22
.... RAT GROWS WEARY OF HIS DEMANDING FAN BASE.
MEET RAT, CREATOR OF "DICKIE THE COCKROACH"!

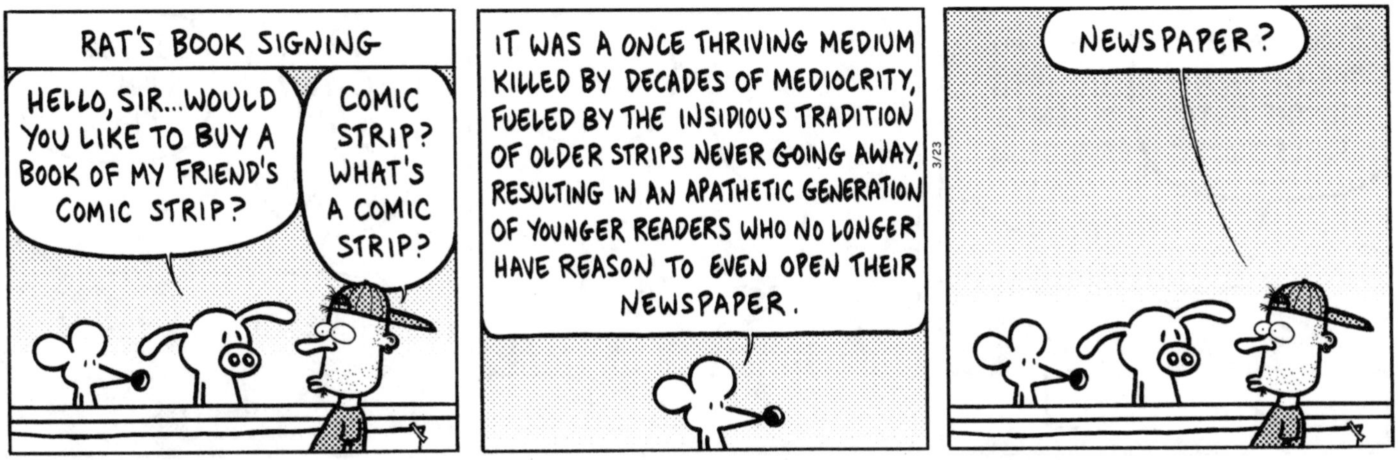
RAT'S BOOK SIGNING
HELLO, SIR... WOULD YOU LIKE TO BUY A BOOK OF MY FRIEND'S COMIC STRIP?
COMIC STRIP? WHAT'S A COMIC STRIP?
IT WAS A ONCE THRIVING MEDIUM KILLED BY DECADES OF MEDIOCRITY, FUELED BY THE INSIDIOUS TRADITION OF OLDER STRIPS NEVER GOING AWAY, RESULTING IN AN APATHETIC GENERATION OF YOUNGER READERS WHO NO LONGER HAVE REASON TO EVEN OPEN THEIR NEWSPAPER.
3/23
NEWSPAPER?

One worrisome topic for a lot of syndicated cartoonists is the lack of young people reading the newspaper. Of course, having a comics page from the 1920s probably doesn't help.

I think I draw myself differently every time I appear in the comic. It probably reflects my level of self-esteem on that particular day. On this day, I apparently felt like an arrogant @$$.

Bill is one of the nicest guys I know, as well as one of the most popular cartoonists today. Whenever I go to a bookstore, I always see one or two kids sitting in the humor aisle reading a *FoxTrot* book. Sometimes I grab it out of their hands and replace it with a *Pearls* book.

I'm often tempted to buy used trophies and fill a room with them. The sadness of it appeals to me.

Look at that *action* in the second panel. Perhaps DC Comics has an opening for me.

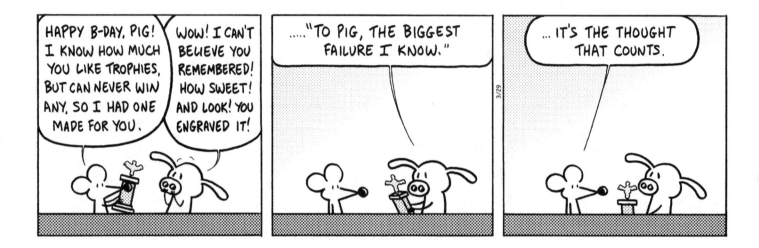

Living in California, I've felt my fair share of earthquakes. I was actually walking across the U.C.-Berkeley campus during the big 1989 Loma Prieta earthquake that postponed the World Series and knocked down part of the Bay Bridge. Since I was walking outside at the time, I didn't really feel the quake, but I knew something was up when the entire Cal men's basketball team came running out of the gym.

In 2005, Bill Amend (*FoxTrot*), Darby Conley (*Get Fuzzy*), and I decided to pull an April Fool's prank by all running the same joke on the same day. Since I was the farthest ahead deadline-wise, I had a bunch of strips that had not yet run, and so I gave Bill and Darby the choice of which one of them they thought would best work with their own characters. They chose this one. So on April 1, 2005, this identical dialogue appeared in *FoxTrot* and *Get Fuzzy*. It generated a huge response from readers, almost all of who seemed to like it. My syndicate, however, was not thrilled, as neither Darby nor I had told them in advance what we were doing.

This one came out of my own life, shortly after my doctor told me that my blood pressure was a little high. But unlike Rat, I now eat tons of broccoli and run.

I worry sometimes about doing jokes like this, given the serious nature of Al-Qaeda and what they do. But I always laugh whenever they show this video of them swinging on monkey bars, so I thought I'd put it in the strip.

This strip ran on April 9, 2005. The next day, Tiger Woods won the Masters. I could not have timed the strip any worse if I had tried.

When I do strips like this, I generally work backward. I have the pun in mind, and then I have to set up how I get to that pun. In this case, the set-up took forever. I generally like to avoid using this many words in a strip.

A friend of mine told me she went to a "life coach," and it just sounded so ridiculous, I thought it would be the perfect job for Rat.

These are the kind of notes I would take if I were a life coach. That is probably why I'm not a life coach.

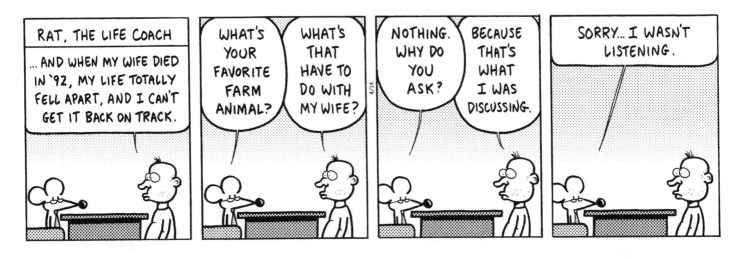

I don't usually do daily strips with this many panels, but I think it worked here.

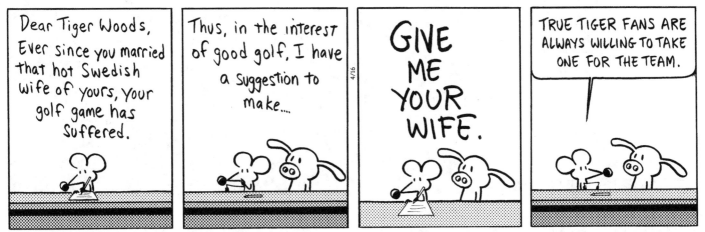

Making my previously mentioned Tiger Woods problem even worse, I had two more of these strips criticizing his play scheduled to run this Saturday and the next Saturday. Given that he was now the 2005 Masters Champion, they were now woefully out-of-date and irrelevant, but it was too late to pull them from publication. This is one of the hazards of having to submit strips so many weeks in advance.

There was a guy at my law firm who had one of these singing fish. It's cute for about four seconds. Then you want to toss the #&@#$@# thing out the window.

Given my ill-fated mention of Denver omelets back in January (see the comments below the January 28, 2005, strip), you'd think I would have learned to avoid Denver omelets altogether. And yet somehow I managed to mention them again. I am not a wise man.

My son really liked this strip and the next one. He seems to like any strip where someone gets smacked in the head.

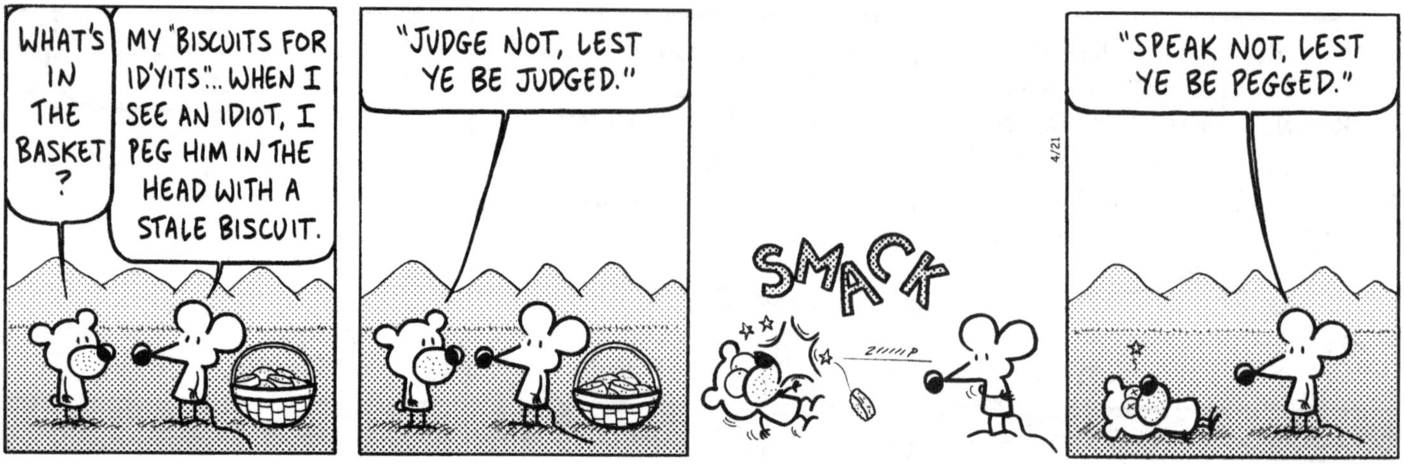
WHAT'S IN THE BASKET?
MY "BISCUITS FOR ID'YITS"... WHEN I SEE AN IDIOT, I PEG HIM IN THE HEAD WITH A STALE BISCUIT.
"JUDGE NOT, LEST YE BE JUDGED."
4/21
SMACK
"SPEAK NOT, LEST YE BE PEGGED."

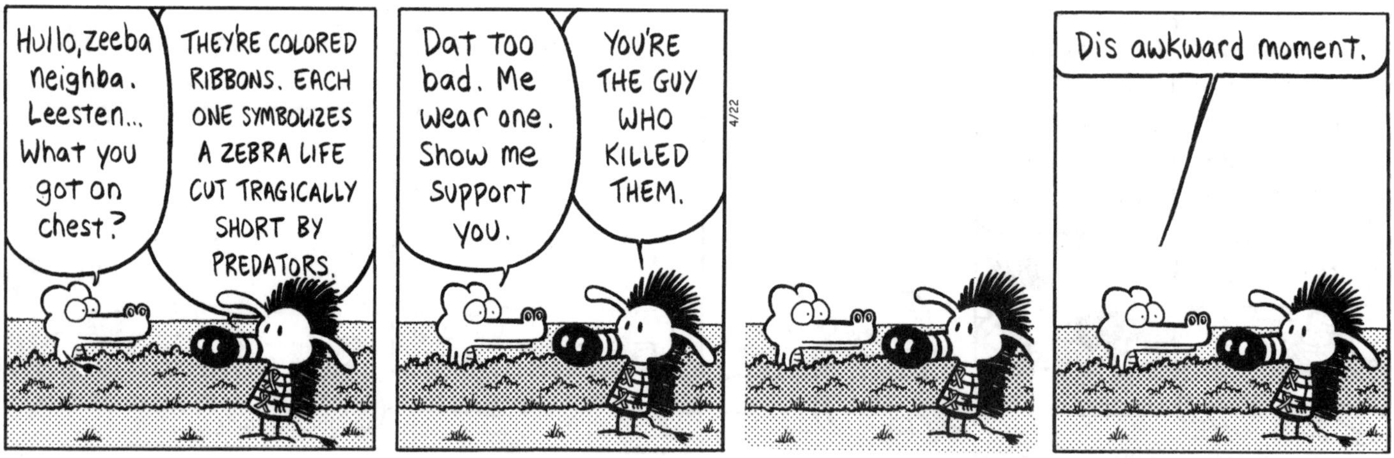
Hullo, zeeba neighba. Leesten... What you got on chest?
THEY'RE COLORED RIBBONS. EACH ONE SYMBOLIZES A ZEBRA LIFE CUT TRAGICALLY SHORT BY PREDATORS.
Dat too bad. Me wear one. Show me support you.
YOU'RE THE GUY WHO KILLED THEM.
4/22
Dis awkward moment.

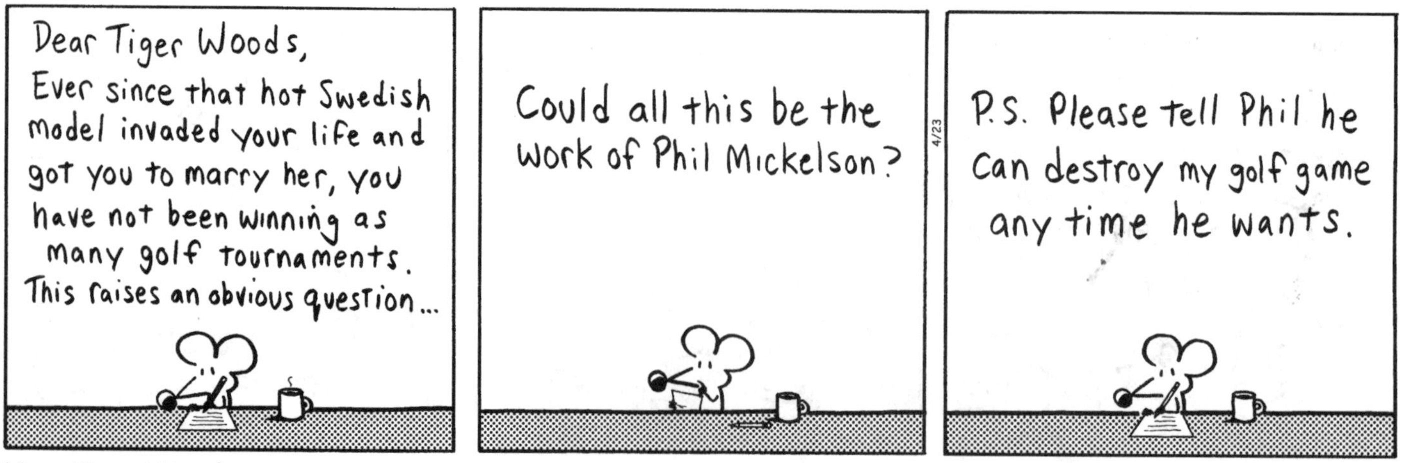
Dear Tiger Woods,
Ever since that hot Swedish model invaded your life and got you to marry her, you have not been winning as many golf tournaments. This raises an obvious question...
Could all this be the work of Phil Mickelson?
4/23
P.S. Please tell Phil he can destroy my golf game any time he wants.

More Tiger Woods pain.

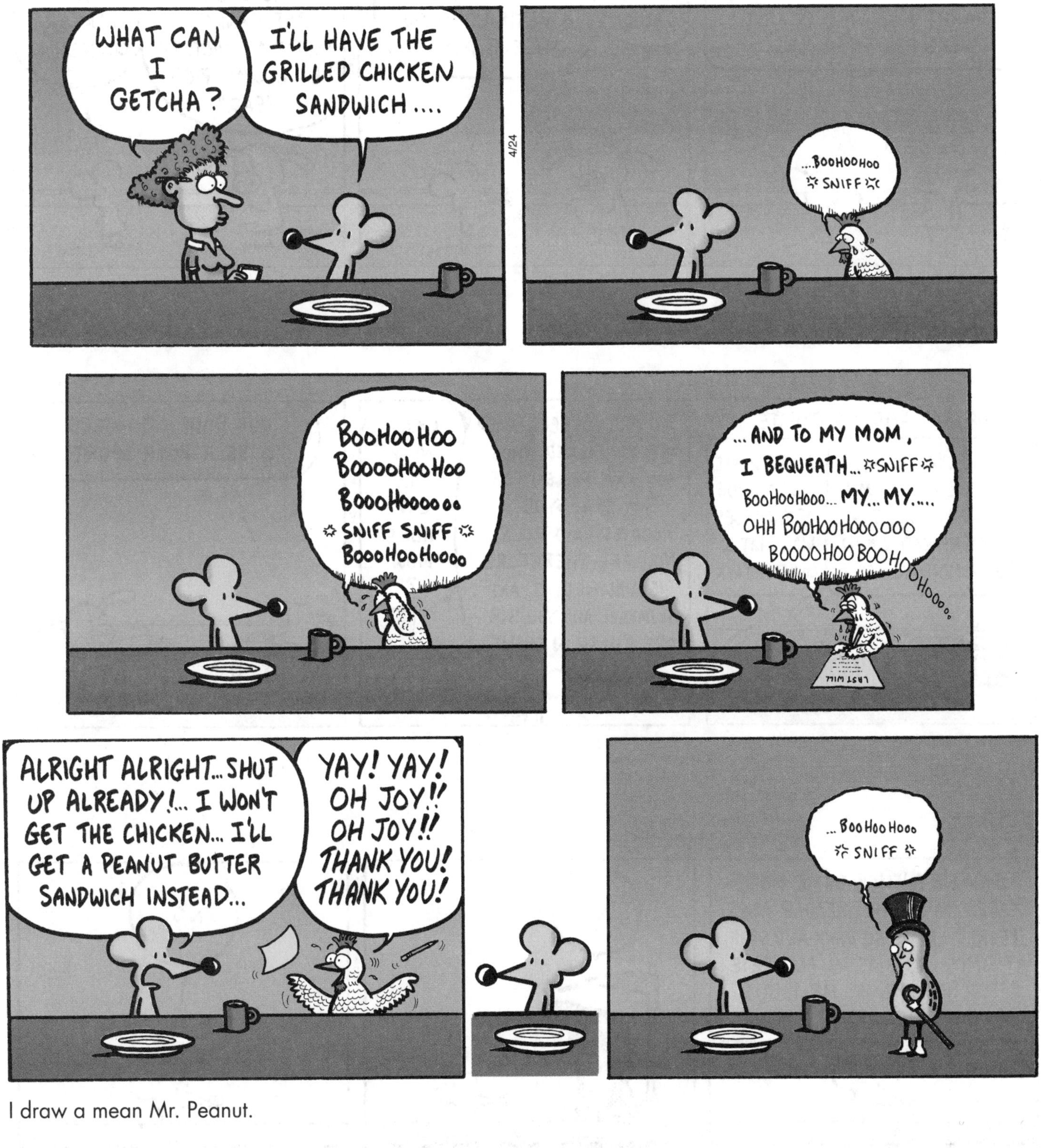
WHAT CAN I GETCHA?
I'LL HAVE THE GRILLED CHICKEN SANDWICH....
4/24
...BOOHOOHOO SNIFF
BOOHOOHOO BOOOOHOOHOO BOOOHOOOOOO SNIFF SNIFF BOOOHOOHOOOO
...AND TO MY MOM, I BEQUEATH... SNIFF BOOHOOHOOO... MY... MY..... OHH BOOHOOHOOOOOO BOOOOHOO BOOHOOHOOooo
LAST WILL
ALRIGHT ALRIGHT... SHUT UP ALREADY!... I WON'T GET THE CHICKEN... I'LL GET A PEANUT BUTTER SANDWICH INSTEAD...
YAY! YAY! OH JOY!! OH JOY!! THANK YOU! THANK YOU!
...BOOHOOHOOO SNIFF

I draw a mean Mr. Peanut.

I frequently wear sweatshirts that have hoods. Lately, I've taken to wearing the hood over my head even when I'm indoors. I've never quite understood why I do it. But now looking back at this strip, I see I am trying to be the Grim Reaper.

PEARLS MAILBAG

TODAY'S LETTER IS FROM GEORGE W. BUSH, OF WASHINGTON, D.C., WHO WRITES, "YOURS IS THE BEST STRIP IN THE WASHINGTON POST...IF POSSIBLE, COULD YOU NAME ONE OF THE CHARACTERS 'GEORGE'?"

NO.....WE CAN'T...AND WHAT ARE YOU GONNA DO ABOUT IT?.....

.... OUR NEXT LETTER IS FROM STEPHAN PASTIS, OF GUANTANAMO BAY, CUBA....

PEARLS MAILBAG

OUR NEXT READER ASKS, "I HEAR SOME CARTOONISTS USE GAG WRITERS.... DO YOU?"... WELL, YES, WE DO USE GAG WRITERS AT 'PEARLS,' BUT BECAUSE WE'RE A NEW STRIP, WE COULDN'T AFFORD MUCH.

THUS, WE GOT A REAL CHEAP GUY FROM PESHTIGO, WISCONSIN, NAMED LARRY.... LARRY IS A FRIENDLESS, HOPELESS SOUL WITH AN UNDERSTANDABLY DARK VIEW OF HUMAN NATURE. HE'S OBSESSED BY DEATH, AND YES, FOR THOSE OF YOU WONDERING, LARRY HAS A BAD MARRIAGE.

HERE'S ONE... A GUY GETS MARRIED... THEN HE DIES.

HEH HEH... GOOD ONE, LARRY.

The truth is that I would never hire a gag writer. To me, the writing is the best part of the job. It would be like someone who loves to catch trout hiring someone to do the fishing for him.

PEARLS MAILBAG

OUR NEXT LETTER IS FOR OUR STRIP'S CREATOR, STEPHAN PASTIS... "STEPHAN, I UNDERSTAND YOU USED TO BE A LAWYER....DO YOU EVER MISS THOSE DAYS?"

HAHAHAHAHAHAH HAHAHAHAHAHAHA SNOOOOOOOORTT HOOHOOHOO HEEHOOHAH

HAHAHAHAHAHA HOOHOOHOOHOO HEEHEEHEE HAHAHAHAH

I THINK THAT'S A "NO."

Look how fat I drew my stomach here. For the record, I do not have a fat stomach. I am a lean, mean fighting machine.

This was one of the most popular croc strips I've done.

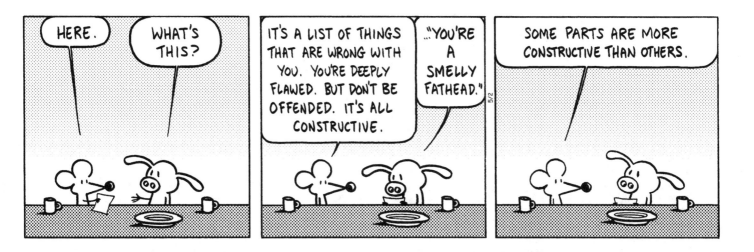

Although I don't sell my strips, I do auction them off for charity now and then. I sold this one on eBay to raise money for Hurricane Katrina victims.

53

This was my parody of the famed artist Christo. His art includes things like sticking lots of umbrellas in the ground and covering stuff in tarps. Then people pay him millions of dollars for it. Some people question whether or not he is truly a genius. I don't. If you can cover stuff in tarps and get millions of dollars for it, you're a genius.

54

I ran this on Mother's Day so that people would think Rat and Pig were paying tribute to their mothers.

I really liked this strip and the next one, but they didn't seem to generate a big reaction.

I'm quite proud of the tire tracks I put on Spiro. Those are some quality tire tracks.

I do everything I can to avoid talking to my neighbors. For example, our garage is out in front of our house, and when I pull my car into the garage, I sometimes see a neighbor across the street who looks like he's going to talk to me when I step out of the car. So instead of getting out of the car, I just sit in there and wait until the automatic garage door fully closes behind me. *Then* I get out.

When I was in junior high, all the fights took place in a church parking lot adjoining the school. If you wanted to fight someone, you just said, "Meet me in the church parking lot after school." Little did I know I would one day work that taunt into a nationally syndicated comic strip.

I did something weird with the clouds in this strip, giving them almost a 3-D effect. If I could remember what it is I did, I'd do it more often.

Sometimes having your dreams come true is worse than having them not come true.

This is one shameful pun. So I ran it on a Saturday. The assumption is that fewer people read the comics on Saturday.

I think one of the funnier parts of the crocodiles is their willingness to kill each other.

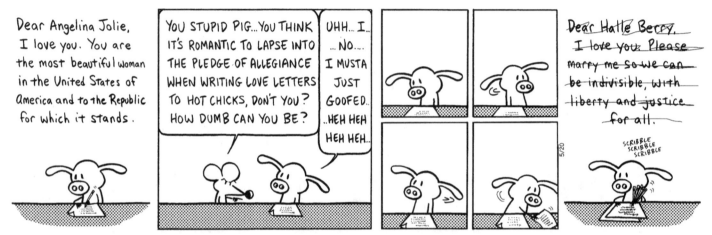

Never heard from Angelina Jolie. Never heard from Halle Berry. One of these days, this trick is gonna work.

The morning this strip appeared, I got an e-mail from Mark Cuban himself, telling me that he loved the strip and that I could make fun of him any time I wanted to. I sent him the original.

Sometimes I write a line I like in my notes and then look for a way to build a strip around it. That was the case here with the line, "Your soul's so dark it smudges mine."

This strip drew complaints from people saying that "gypsy" jokes are actually a slight on Romanians. I told them that I had no intention to make fun of Romanian people and added that if I ever *did* intend on making fun of Romanian people, they'd know.

This "end o' the world" box turned out to be very popular with readers.

I got the idea for this strip from watching my friend, Emilio. Whenever we're at a bar and he tells a joke that bombs, he leans into his beer as though it was a microphone and says, "Please drive home safely," like he's a cheesy stand-up comic finishing his act.

Maybe it's a sign of how juvenile my humor is, but there's something about Port-A-Potties that I just find very funny.

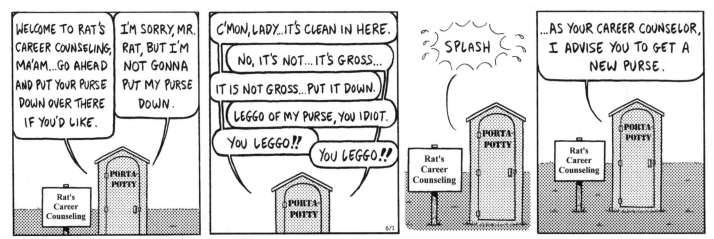

This is one of the only strips I've ever done where no characters appear. In fact, other than the Jerusalem bus strip, I can't think of any others.

Given the subject matter of this one, I was a little worried about the reaction it would get, but the complaints were minimal.

The truth is I do show Rat driving a car now and then. Maybe Pig owns it.

As an attorney, I never told a "your mama" joke in court. But I wanted to.

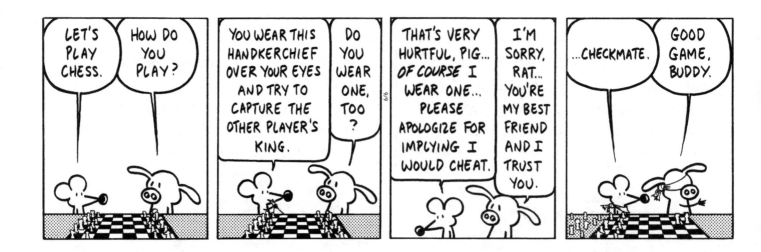

That's my rendering of our very own fax machine in that last panel. Again, it's inside knowledge like this that makes these treasuries worth the extra money.

The oar. The raft. The harpoon. Why, this comic is a tour de force of artistic greatness.

The truth is that I've never understood Bill Watterson's stand against licensing. While no one wants their characters exploited in a way that undermines who they are, I don't see anything wrong with putting them on a T-shirt.

If you look at those book spines carefully, you'll see the names of my family members, relatives, and friends, as well as the titles of books I like and comics I like.

I'm with Rat here. I get no comfort in knowing that my deceased relatives are watching me. More than anything, it worries me.

Believe it or not, shooting someone in the comics can actually be a problem. Some papers won't even run the strip. It's strange that Bugs Bunny and Daffy Duck could get away with more stuff in the 1940s than I can now.

Every now and then, I tried to bring back Wee Bear, but he just wasn't that popular with most people.

The crocs' most popular line seems to be "Hulloooo, zeeba neighba," but the line I like best is "Peese shut mouf."

That recliner took me so long to draw that I just cut and pasted it into the next two panels. Artistic purists, look away.

This one drew complaints from people angry over my making light of hostage situations. It's so odd to me which topics provoke complaints and which don't.

This tree series originally had three strips in it, but just before they were set to run, I decided I really didn't like any of them. They just seemed like they were trying too hard to make a point and they weren't very well drawn. I thought about pulling them all, but three strips is a lot to lose, so in the end I compromised and just nixed one of them. You can see the nixed strip in the "Not Ready for Prime Time Comic Strips" section of this book.

DEAR MR. COMIC SYNDICATE EDITOR, I HAVE NOTICED THAT IN THE LAST COUPLE YEARS, COMIC STRIP SYNDICATES HAVE RELEASED COMIC STRIP AFTER COMIC STRIP THAT ARE MEANT SOLELY TO APPEAL TO ONE SPECIFIC MINORITY GROUP OR ANOTHER.

IN DOING SO, THEY HAVE IGNORED THE FACT THAT MANY OF THESE STRIPS SIMPLY ARE NOT FUNNY.

CALL ME NUTS, BUT I THINK A COMIC STRIP SHOULD BE JUDGED UPON WHETHER OR NOT IT IS FUNNY.

AS SUCH, I THINK THAT BOTH COMIC STRIP ARTISTS AND SYNDICATES NEED TO STOP TAKING THE EASY WAY OUT BY MANUFACTURING THESE FORCED DEMOGRAPHIC STRIPS THAT GARNER COMPARATIVELY EASY NEWSPAPER SALES AND INSTEAD, TAKE A CHANCE ON A STRIP BASED SOLELY UPON ITS LEVEL OF COMEDIC CONTENT.

ONLY THEN CAN THE "FUNNIES" PAGE RETURN TO THE BUSINESS OF BEING FUNNY...

6/26

P.S. ENCLOSED PLEASE FIND MY COMIC STRIP, "BELA, THE ONE-LEGGED ALBANIAN BLIND BOY WHOSE DIVORCED PARENTS SPEAK FLUENT SPANISH."

...IT'S MUY BUENO.

This strip generated a couple of angry e-mails from syndicated cartoonists who do such demographic strips. One of them even went on to criticize me in one of his Sunday strips a couple months later. Their point was that instead of going after them, I should go after the old legacy strips, which in their opinion *really* aren't funny. I told them I poke fun at the older strips all the time. The next week of *Pearls* strips proved my point.

"I'm sorry, Osama, but at the end of grace, we say, 'Amen,' not 'Death to America.'"

I think this is probably the most popular series I've ever done, and man, was I worried about it. Bringing Osama Bin Laden into the strip is dangerous enough, as many people view it as making light of terrorism. But throwing him into a family strip that is beloved by millions of older readers is doubly dangerous. As it turned out, the risk paid off and the series was amazingly popular. And proving yet again what a great sport he is, Bil Keane asked for the original of this first strip, which I gave to him.

"...And when your father leaves for work, we give him hugs and kisses. We do not call him 'The Great Satan' and place a fatwa upon his head."

Bil Keane once asked me why it was that every time I do a *Family Circus* parody I draw the characters as they *used* to be drawn back in the 1960s. I told him that when I do the parodies, I try to base the drawing on an actual *Family Circus* cartoon, and the only *Family Circus* books I own are from the 1960s, when the characters (especially the parents) looked different.

"...Culture *smulture*, you weirdo...My wife's got a bootylicious bod and DARN it, I want to see it."

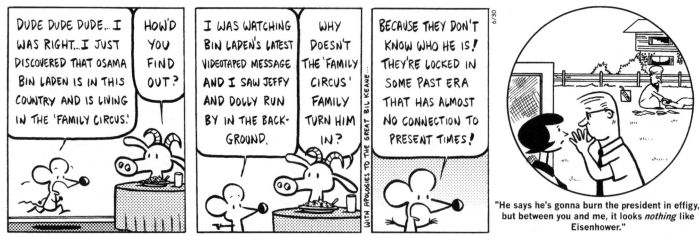

"He says he's gonna burn the president in effigy, but between you and me, it looks *nothing* like Eisenhower."

In the original of this *Family Circus* I believe the father was whispering to his wife about something Billy was doing in the backyard. I just removed Billy and replaced him with Osama and a can of gasoline.

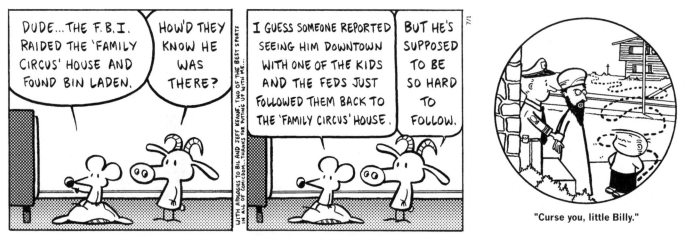

"Curse you, little Billy."

You can't do a week of *Family Circus* parodies without making a dotted line joke.

Guantanamo Bay, Cuba

"On a positive note, this should give us a whole BUNCH of new material."

Of all the strips in this series, this was the one I was the most worried about. It's one thing to parody Osama and the *Family Circus*. But to then add Guantanamo Bay to the mix and show the kids hooded like prisoners is really pushing the limit. Not surprisingly, the strip drew a number of complaints. Nevertheless, I think it's my favorite strip of the week.

78

The huge, oversized speech balloon in the last panel here is a hint that something had to be edited out. And what had to be edited out was the original quote I was using. Originally, I had the character in the last panel giving the prison official's famous speech from the movie, *Cool Hand Luke*. This was the speech that begins with the line, "What we've got here is failure to communicate." But just before it was going to run, I showed the strip to a number of people and very few of them knew the quote. So rather than confuse everyone, I just changed it to this more famous quote from *Terminator 2*. The original of this strip is in the "Not Ready for Prime Time Comic Strips" section of this book.

I'm not sure why Pig is obsessed with Cher. I guess I just thought it was funny to portray her as an omnipotent presence.

This seemed like a funny joke until I had to actually draw all those pickle jars. I will never set a joke in a grocery store aisle again.

Whenever I draw something for the first time, I tend to overdraw it. That's the case here with the Uzi the bull is holding in the last panel. It has way more detail than anything else in the strip. Most things I draw are really simplified, but I can't seem to simplify them until I have a rough idea of how to actually draw them first.

We don't have any purple houses in our neighborhood, but we do have barking dogs. In fact, there's one next door named "November" that barks whenever his owner leaves. Every now and then I open the window of the room I draw in and yell out, "November, be quiet!" To the casual passerby, it appears like I'm cursing out a month.

The minute I learned that crocs carry their newborns in their mouth, I knew I had to do a strip about it. I think this is one of my favorite croc strips.

The idea with the antelopes was to create an animal that the crocodiles could actually catch.

The guy here is supposed to be me during my lawyer days. I named him "Jim" to throw you off the trail.

WHO'S AT THE FRONT DOOR?

YOUR CROCODILE NEIGHBORS...THEY'RE BOBBING FOR APPLES AND WANT TO KNOW IF YOU'D JOIN THEM.

7/14

PIG...ONE OF THOSE CROCODILES IS WAITING AT THE BOTTOM OF THAT WATER....IF I STICK MY HEAD IN THERE, HE'LL BITE IT AND THEY'LL EAT ME AND I'LL DIE.

IS THAT A NO?

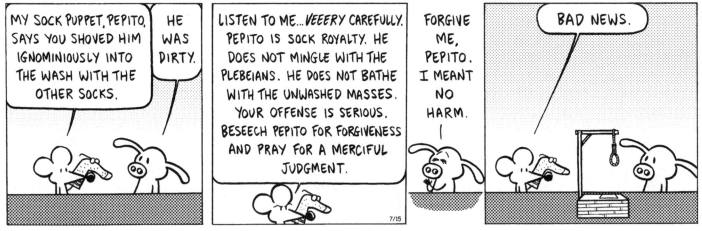

MY SOCK PUPPET, PEPITO, SAYS YOU SHOVED HIM IGNOMINIOUSLY INTO THE WASH WITH THE OTHER SOCKS.

HE WAS DIRTY.

LISTEN TO ME... VEEERY CAREFULLY. PEPITO IS SOCK ROYALTY. HE DOES NOT MINGLE WITH THE PLEBEIANS. HE DOES NOT BATHE WITH THE UNWASHED MASSES. YOUR OFFENSE IS SERIOUS. BESEECH PEPITO FOR FORGIVENESS AND PRAY FOR A MERCIFUL JUDGMENT.

7/15

FORGIVE ME, PEPITO. I MEANT NO HARM.

BAD NEWS.

Pepito is Rat's evil alter ego.

MY SOCK PUPPET, PEPITO, SAYS YOU'RE THE TYPE OF GUY WHO WOULD QUESTION HIS CREDIBILITY, FORCING HIM TO BEAT YOU ABOUT THE HEAD... IS PEPITO TELLING ME THE TRUTH?

7/16

GEE... I DON'T THINK SO.

....BEHOLD. A PROPHET.

Rat is Stephan's evil alter ego.

Pig's obsession with Cher continues.

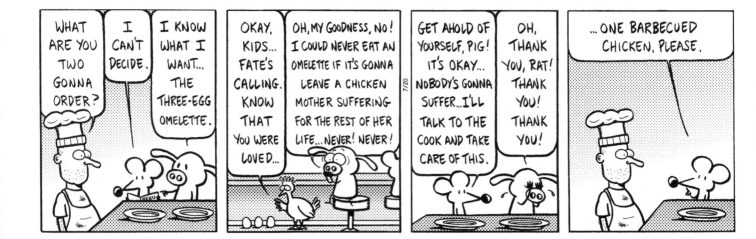

86

For those of you wondering, Pig is supposed to be waving in that last panel. He does not have six arms.

Years ago, I walked into the Hard Rock Cafe in London not knowing that it was actually closed to the public that day because they were taping some press conference. As it turned out, the place was filled with rock stars, including Lou Reed, Bryan Adams, and Chrissie Hynde. Eventually, I noticed that you had to have a special pass around your neck to be in the room. To hide the fact that I wasn't wearing one, I leaned my chest into a pole. I watched the entire press conference from behind that pole.

I can't draw a cliff to save my life, so for that second-to-last panel, I looked at a *Calvin and Hobbes* book. If I ever meet Bill Watterson, I will give him a royalty check.

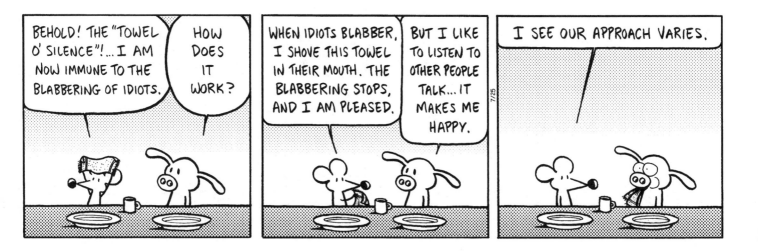

There's a syndicated cartoonist who occasionally posts on internet message boards asserting things "without fear of contradiction." The phrase struck me as funny, so I gave it to the character in the first panel.

This strip came from my son Tom. We were at a restaurant in Bodega Bay, California, and he saw a sign advertising a "crab feed." He got really excited and said he wanted to go, which struck me as odd because he doesn't eat crab. When I asked him why he wanted to go, he said he thought it would be really fun to feed the crabs. And thus, this strip was born.

A *Pearls* strip with only three spoken words. A rarity.

90

I really do have a friend named John Patzakis, but I'm the guy who wrote and drew this strip. Pretty much everything in it is true, except for the fact that I did not have to wait until college to kiss a girl (but it was close).

Some people are troubled by the fact that Pig eats food that comes from pigs. But even Pig has to have at least one weakness.

Sometimes I look at my strip and can really see the influence of *Peanuts*. This is one of those instances. The way Pig is rejected reminds me of the way Charlie Brown used to get rejected by his peers.

I was a little worried about the graphic nature of this one (showing the smooshed Tinkerbell in the last panel). But it made me laugh, so I ran it.

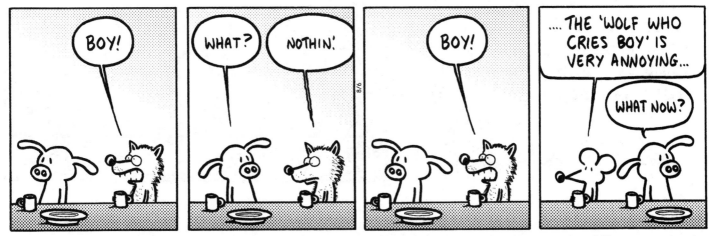

This is another really old strip that I didn't run until a couple years after it was drawn. I used a different pen back then, so the linework looks much different.

Whenever I draw a strip, the first thing I do is draw the pencil guidelines that the dialogue will be written on. That way the words all appear straight. This is one of the rare instances where I didn't use any guidelines, which makes the words appear much more crooked. I did this because I thought it better conveyed the madness and passion in Beethoven's speech.

Josh and Ben are my wife Staci's cousins. I see them once a year for Christmas. That is once a year too much.

The squirrel's lines here are taken from the Book of Revelation.

Someone from Home Depot's headquarters contacted me about this strip and asked if they could have a print of it. Apparently, they keep a collection of all the comics that reference them.

I really do find it fascinating that we now know so much about complete strangers and so little about our own neighbors. I guess if I ever talked to my neighbors, I'd know something about them. But that's asking too much.

Have you ever noticed that every single airline pilot in the United States seems to have a Southern accent? Someone needs to look into that.

"Blah blah blah whatever" is my standard comeback to anyone who disagrees with me.

We recently got a couple of hamsters. I build huge Lego forts for them to run through.

We also recently got a couple of fish. But I do not build Lego forts for them.

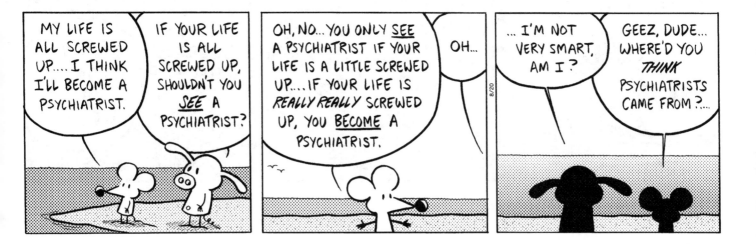

My son and daughter watch SpongeBob endlessly.

This was originally going to be a weeklong series, but I didn't like the rest of the strips I had written, so I just drew this one.

Pig is the heart and soul of the strip.

One day I want to somehow write Humpty Dumpty into the strip as a semi-regular character. A talking egg who dies tragically is the pinnacle of comedy.

This was the first of a weeklong series that I was very worried about. The reason for my concern was that for whatever reason, the topics of guns and gun control are relatively taboo on the American comics page. Some newspaper editors won't even run strips that relate to gun violence. Consequently, my syndicate was also concerned. But the difficulty here was that this involved a whole week of dailies, and I didn't want to lose six strips. So I compromised by breaking them up and running them one at a time over the next year, mostly on Saturdays, when fewer people read the comics.

To this day, I have trouble remembering that when someone says the "18th century," they are referring to the 1700s. It always causes me to pause and think. Someone needs to fix all that.

I don't know how people lived without Google. Whenever I need to look up a fact for my strip or see what something looks like, I go immediately to Google and it's all instantly there. Prior to the internet and Google, cartoonists had to keep volumes and volumes of reference books.

Lorena and Pete are two of my friends from college. They're married to each other. I'm not sure if they were flattered by this.

I was going to name the stuck crocodile after one of my syndicate's salesmen, but I didn't want him to think I was calling him fat. Thus, I refrained. You've got to be nice to your salesmen. They put you in papers. Calling them fat is a bad idea.

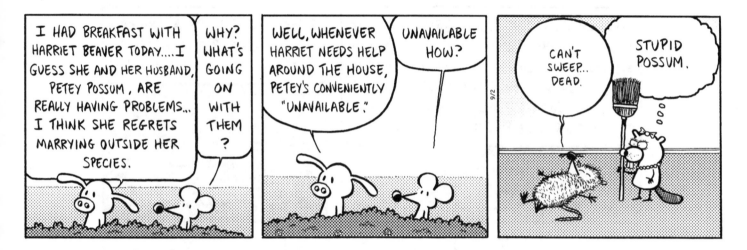

105

Little did you know that Rat has lips. Quite big lips, as it turns out.

A lot of readers responded favorably to this one. You can't go wrong making fun of stupid people.

From the earliest days of the strip, Rat has been eating Pig's friends.

Oh man, this is a weak one. Hence, I buried it on a Saturday. I've talked to other cartoonists about whether or not they bury their weaker strips on Saturday and learned it is a common practice. As one said to me, "Imagine the poor person who only reads the comics on Saturday."

If you look at the top line of dialogue in the second panel, you'll see large margins on the left and right. This almost always means that something got deleted at the request of my syndicate. And that is the case here. Originally, the line was, "No *straight* man is friends with a woman . . . " I included the word "straight" so that I wouldn't get e-mail saying that there were plenty of gay men who were friends with women. But believe it or not, the word "straight" created problems, because the opposite of straight is gay, and the latter can generate complaints, particularly in a Sunday strip, when presumably more kids read the paper. The interesting part is that when my syndicate contacted me about the strip, I was sure they were going to complain about the use of the word "eunuch." But no, "eunuch" was fine. Only "straight" had to go.

I have to say I know next to nothing about Clay Aiken, other than that he was a person who was on *American Idol*, a show I've never even watched. But after doing this strip, I learned that there are lots of people in this country who ARE Clay Aiken fans and if you write a strip where you include his name, they will write to you and ask you all sorts of questions about how you first got into Clay and what Clay means to you. Scary stuff. Enough to convince you never to mention his name again.

The duck character here was somewhere between his initial persona of a violent guard duck and his later persona as a duck in the army. I guess I wasn't quite sure what to do with him and I was sort of looking for direction. Looking back on it, I don't think robbing banks would be a natural part of his character.

On the exact same day this strip appeared, Wiley Miller (creator of the great strip, *Non Sequitur*) ran almost the identical joke in his strip, where he had a bird in court being labeled a flight risk. Everyone thought we had planned it in advance, but we hadn't. It was just one of those improbable coincidences that occasionally happens in the comics.

If I name a character "Timmy," it's almost certain he will die.

This is one directly out of my life. I took my daughter to an Applebee's and the guy in the booth next to us wouldn't shut up. Little does he know he became a comic strip character.

Another strip in the vein of the original "Box O' Stupid People" strip that I did in my first year of syndication. I don't know what it is about me and shoving people into boxes. Maybe it's because a box is the only shape I can draw.

When I first heard that there was going to be a celebration on the comics page for the seventy-fifth anniversary of the comic strip *Blondie*, and that I wasn't invited to participate, I knew I had to participate.

While I know most of the creators whose work I parody, I've never met the *Blondie* creators. So I don't actually know how they view *Pearls*, or if they've even read it.

In the original of this strip, I was not saying, "Dilbert is a stud!" in that last panel. Instead, I was commenting on the physical appearance of a cartoonist whose name I cannot say. The reason I cannot say is that before the strip ran, I called him/her and mentioned that I was doing a strip where he/she was described as playing "naked Twister." For the first time in my career, someone flat out told me no. They did not want their name mentioned in that regard. So I changed the line to what you see now.

   In a subsequent and scary twist, just two days before the modified strip was to run, I got a call from a newspaper editor I know saying how much they loved my reference to said cartoonist (editors usually see the strips in advance of their publication). I was confused because we had changed the strip to delete that person's name. It was then that I learned that my syndicate had sent out the original strip, unchanged. I quickly had to get on the phone to my syndicate, who in turn had to call every paper I appear in and get the strip removed. Had that one newspaper editor not called to tell me the strip was funny, the strip would have run unedited in every single newspaper.

I sent the original of this strip to Berkeley Breathed, the creator of *Bloom County*. Unbelievably, he sent me an original *Bloom County* strip in return. I could not believe his generosity. Every time I look at the strip framed on my wall, I'm shocked that it's there. *Bloom County* had a huge influence on me as a cartoonist.

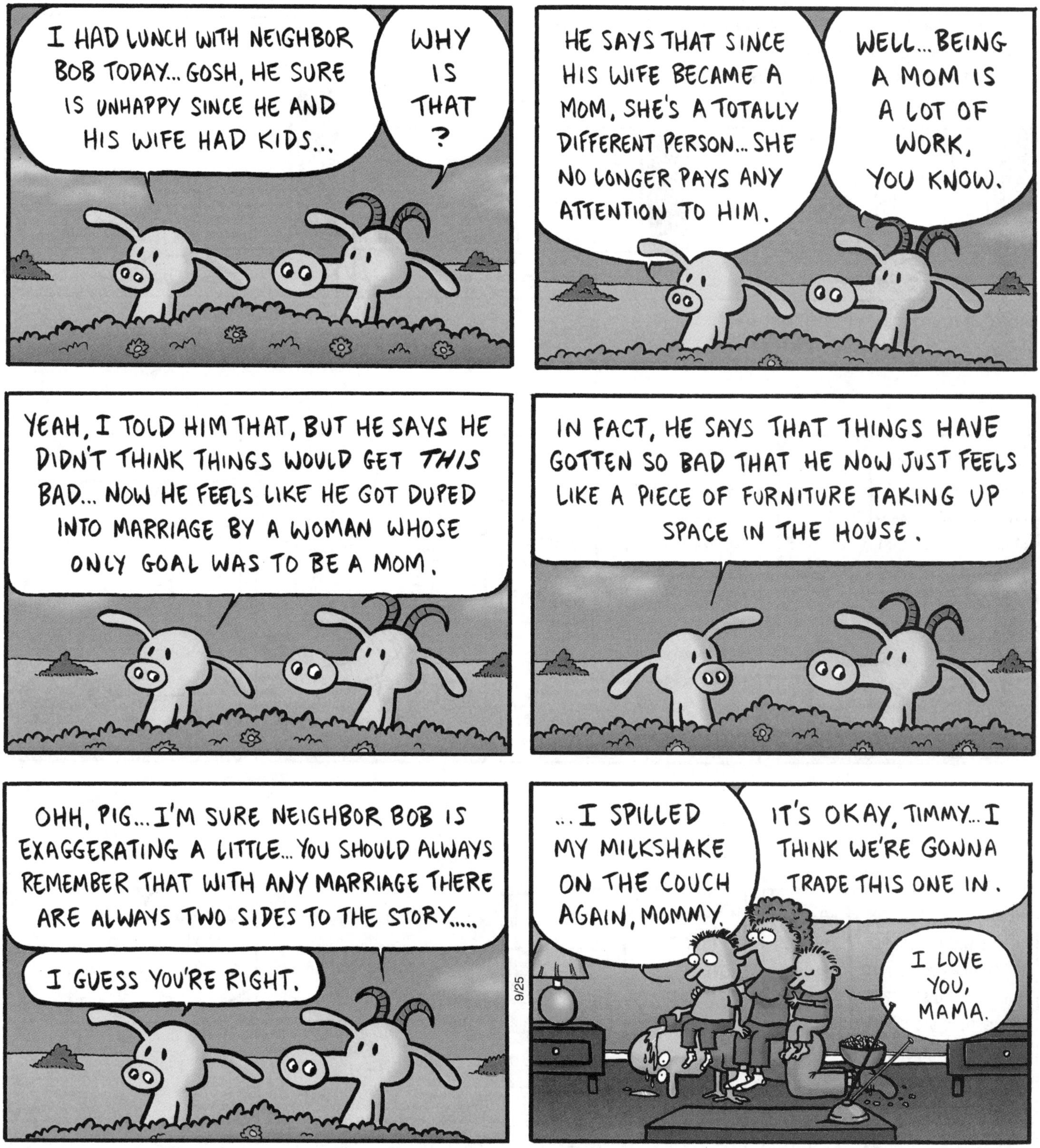
I HAD LUNCH WITH NEIGHBOR BOB TODAY... GOSH, HE SURE IS UNHAPPY SINCE HE AND HIS WIFE HAD KIDS...
WHY IS THAT?
HE SAYS THAT SINCE HIS WIFE BECAME A MOM, SHE'S A TOTALLY DIFFERENT PERSON... SHE NO LONGER PAYS ANY ATTENTION TO HIM.
WELL... BEING A MOM IS A LOT OF WORK, YOU KNOW.
YEAH, I TOLD HIM THAT, BUT HE SAYS HE DIDN'T THINK THINGS WOULD GET *THIS* BAD... NOW HE FEELS LIKE HE GOT DUPED INTO MARRIAGE BY A WOMAN WHOSE ONLY GOAL WAS TO BE A MOM.
IN FACT, HE SAYS THAT THINGS HAVE GOTTEN SO BAD THAT HE NOW JUST FEELS LIKE A PIECE OF FURNITURE TAKING UP SPACE IN THE HOUSE.
OHH, PIG... I'M SURE NEIGHBOR BOB IS EXAGGERATING A LITTLE... YOU SHOULD ALWAYS REMEMBER THAT WITH ANY MARRIAGE THERE ARE ALWAYS TWO SIDES TO THE STORY.....
I GUESS YOU'RE RIGHT.
9/25
... I SPILLED MY MILKSHAKE ON THE COUCH AGAIN, MOMMY.
IT'S OKAY, TIMMY... I THINK WE'RE GONNA TRADE THIS ONE IN.
I LOVE YOU, MAMA.

More of the duck in transition.

116

For me, this was the best of the antelope strips.

I'm not sure how a sock pulls off a spontaneous smile like that.

This is one of those strips where the crocs drop most of their "R"s when they speak ("foh," "fwee," "fwench"). They don't do that anymore, except with the words "zeeba" and "neighba." It just sounded too baby-like.

118

Let me just tell you, it took about two hours for me to draw that stupid engorged duck in that last panel. These strips always seem like a good idea when I write them, but then when I have to draw them, it's a whole different story. Cartooning would be a much easier profession if it weren't for all that cartooning.

After this strip appeared, I got an e-mail from a reader who had taken Rat's quote and superimposed it over a tranquil nature scene, creating a very funny looking "inspirational" poster. It was hilarious to actually see.

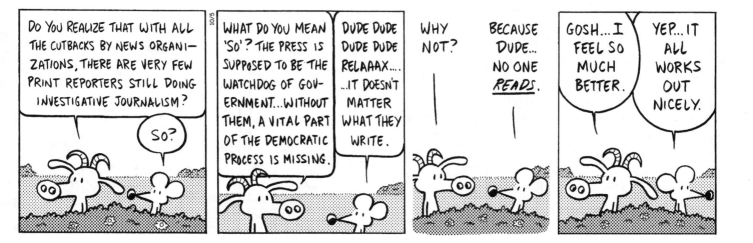

This is a depiction of my best friend, Emilio. I think he's sensitive about his hair receding, so I drew his hairline *really* receding. To make him extra happy, I drew him fat.

The same fan mentioned in the comment to the 10/4 strip turned this quote into an "inspirational" poster also. It was even funnier than the last one.

On the days that I write and draw *Pearls*, I make myself almost impossible to reach. I turn off the cell phone completely. It's the best part of the week.

Another case of where Rat and I differ. I actually go to the gym and run three days a week.

This strip drew complaints from some women. I was pretty sure it would, but it made me laugh, so I ran it. Strips like this are a balance between funniness and offensiveness. If they're funny enough (to me), but a little offensive, I run them. If they're just so-so funny with a high risk of offensiveness, I don't.

The "Ron" here is "Ron O'Neal," a salesman for my syndicate, United Feature Syndicate. Ron has successfully put *Pearls* in newspapers all around the western United States. If you're a syndicated cartoonist, your salespeople are absolutely critical to your success. This is especially so when you're a younger cartoonist with an "edgy" strip. These salespeople have to convince newspaper editors (many of whom are very comfortable with the status quo of older comics) to take a chance on a younger strip, a step that is almost certain to at least temporarily trigger the ire of older readers. I am very lucky to have some of the best salespeople in the business working for my syndicate. You wouldn't know it by my depiction of them as annoying pudgy guys who get shoved through walls, but I am.

122

This strip was the result of a contest that was run by a newspaper in Oregon. The newspaper asked readers to send in ideas for a *Pearls* strip. Most of the submissions involved readers writing entire strips (i.e., all of the characters' dialogue). I didn't really like those, though, because it always feels unnatural for me to hear dialogue written for the characters by someone else. But one woman simply suggested adding a frog as a character. I declared her the winner and drew this strip.

123

Every time I pull up to a drive-through window and pay for the food, I'm tempted to do this. I'm not sure why. I just think it would be so confusing for the drive-through employee to see someone who had just paid for food race off before actually receiving it.

After I was done with this series, I really regretted it. I thought it was way too long (nine days) and worse, it centered around a character (Wee Bear) who wasn't that popular. But unbelievably, the series drew a lot of positive feedback, proving once again that I have no idea in advance what strips will and will not work.

The Fitzgerald quote is from the end of *The Great Gatsby*, a book I try to re-read every couple years.

I was a little worried that this strip and the next strip would offend readers of the *Salt Lake Tribune*, where *Pearls* runs. As it turned out, there were complaints, but not a lot.

This strip was originally scheduled to run in October 2004, but in June 2004, Ronald Reagan died. Believe it or not, a strip like this would trigger an avalanche of angry mail if it appeared so close in time to his death, so I pulled it and ran it a year later.

I think these last few strips are what made this series work. They were sort of touching, I guess, at least for a *Pearls* strip. I was kind of hoping Willie Mays would see them because the strip runs in the *San Francisco Chronicle* and I know that he lives in the Bay Area. But I don't know if he did or not.

128

This was a really popular strip. I think Scott Adams (*Dilbert*) even linked to it in his blog one day.

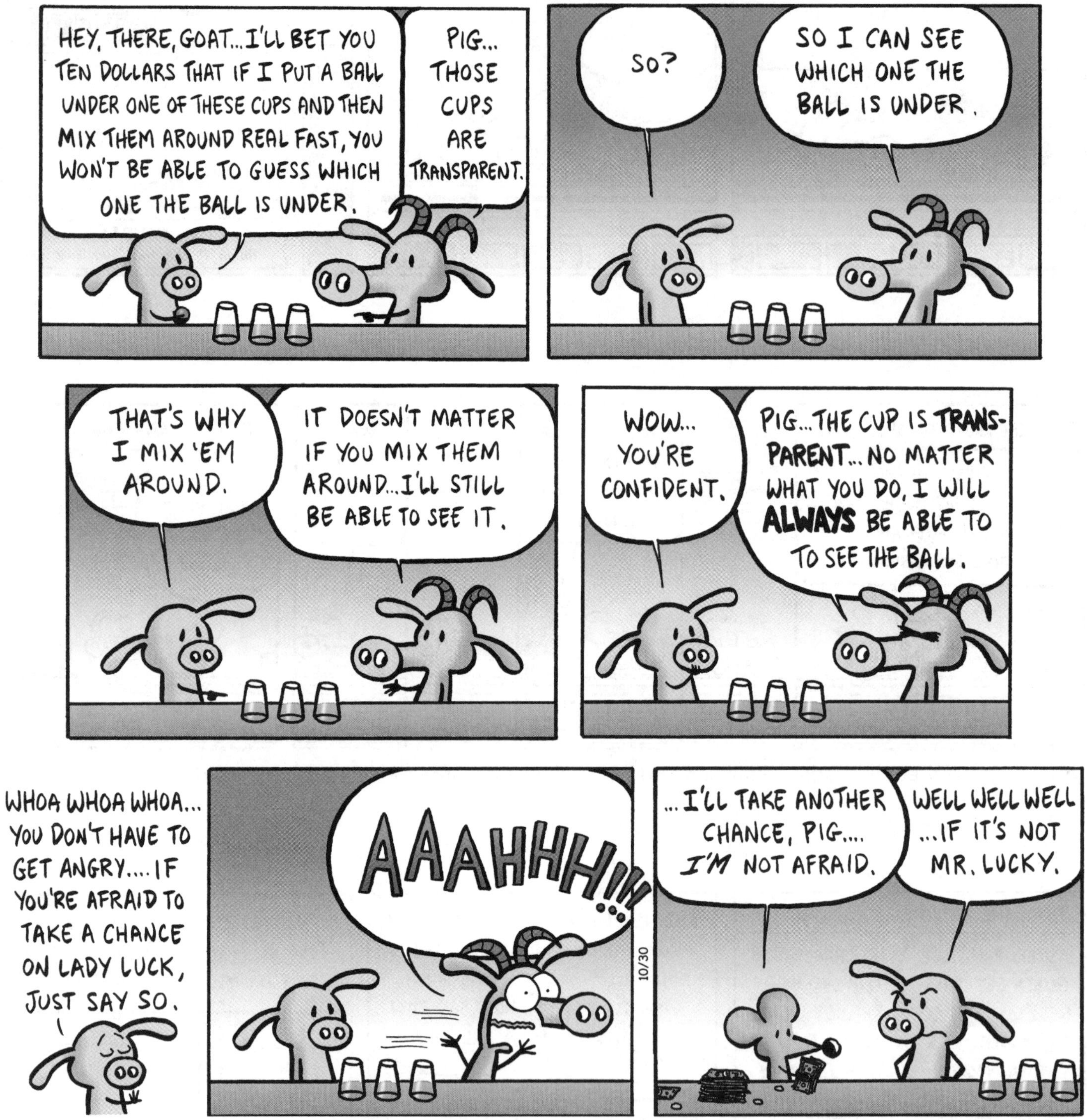
HEY, THERE, GOAT... I'LL BET YOU TEN DOLLARS THAT IF I PUT A BALL UNDER ONE OF THESE CUPS AND THEN MIX THEM AROUND REAL FAST, YOU WON'T BE ABLE TO GUESS WHICH ONE THE BALL IS UNDER.
PIG... THOSE CUPS ARE TRANSPARENT.
SO?
SO I CAN SEE WHICH ONE THE BALL IS UNDER.
THAT'S WHY I MIX 'EM AROUND.
IT DOESN'T MATTER IF YOU MIX THEM AROUND... I'LL STILL BE ABLE TO SEE IT.
WOW... YOU'RE CONFIDENT.
PIG... THE CUP IS **TRANS-PARENT**... NO MATTER WHAT YOU DO, I WILL **ALWAYS** BE ABLE TO TO SEE THE BALL.
WHOA WHOA WHOA... YOU DON'T HAVE TO GET ANGRY.... IF YOU'RE AFRAID TO TAKE A CHANCE ON LADY LUCK, JUST SAY SO.
AAAHHH!!!
10/30
... I'LL TAKE ANOTHER CHANCE, PIG.... *I'M* NOT AFRAID.
WELL WELL WELL ...IF IT'S NOT MR. LUCKY.

If you look at the cover of the last collection, *The Sopratos*, you will see poor, dead Willy lying on the ground.

I think Rat looks good as a surgeon.

Sadly, I'm the only person in the *Pearls* Character Design Department, and I weigh a lot more than these guys.

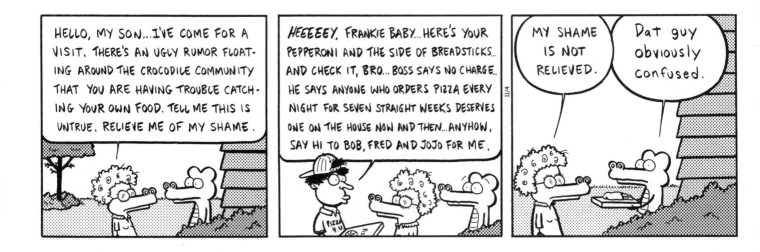

After I drew this, I thought it came out a little harsher than I intended, with Rat just hitting Pig in the face like that. So I ran it on a Saturday.

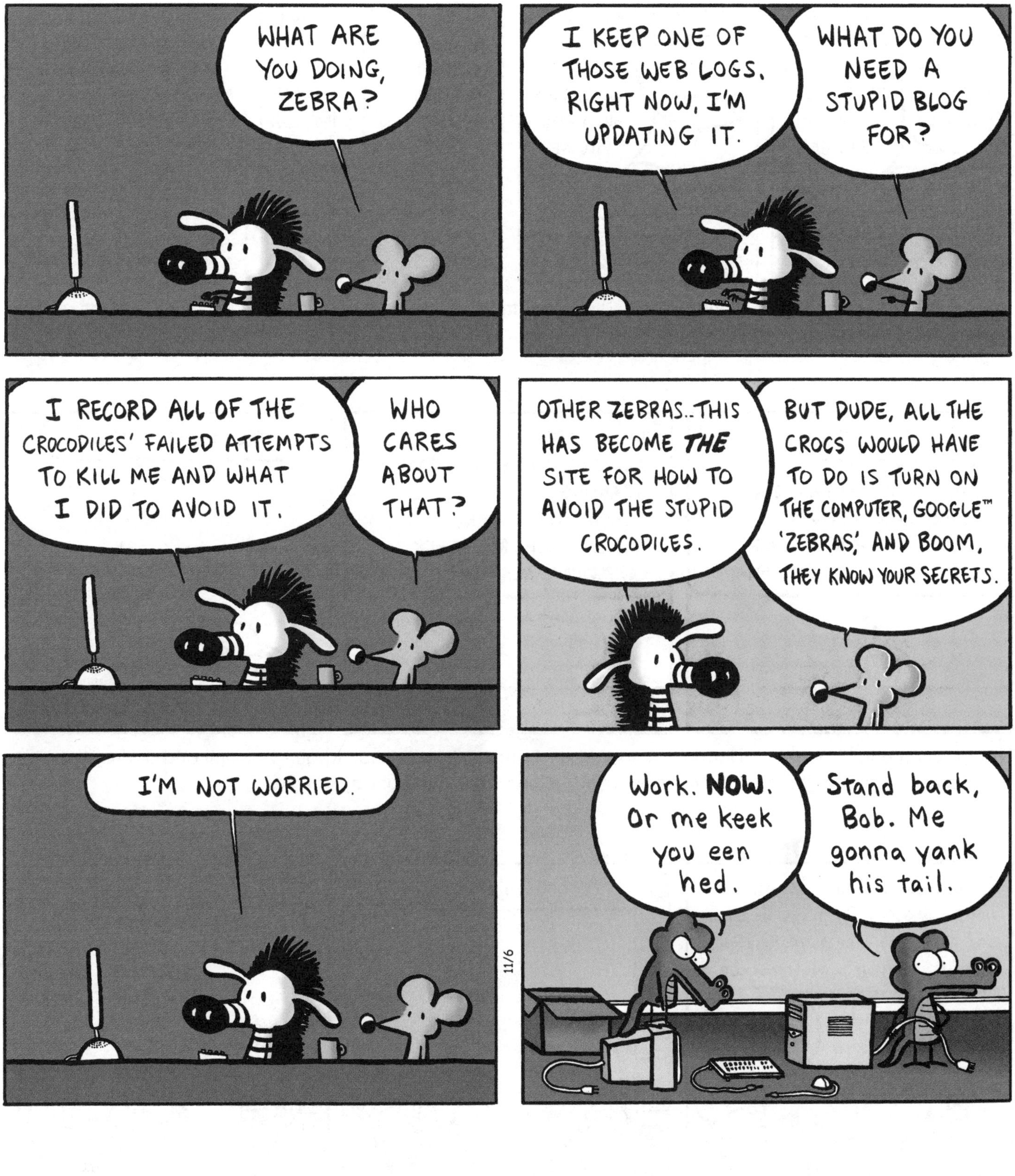
WHAT ARE YOU DOING, ZEBRA?
I KEEP ONE OF THOSE WEB LOGS. RIGHT NOW, I'M UPDATING IT.
WHAT DO YOU NEED A STUPID BLOG FOR?
I RECORD ALL OF THE CROCODILES' FAILED ATTEMPTS TO KILL ME AND WHAT I DID TO AVOID IT.
WHO CARES ABOUT THAT?
OTHER ZEBRAS...THIS HAS BECOME **THE** SITE FOR HOW TO AVOID THE STUPID CROCODILES.
BUT DUDE, ALL THE CROCS WOULD HAVE TO DO IS TURN ON THE COMPUTER, GOOGLE™ 'ZEBRAS,' AND BOOM, THEY KNOW YOUR SECRETS.
I'M NOT WORRIED.
11/6
Work. **NOW**. Or me keek you een hed.
Stand back, Bob. Me gonna yank his tail.

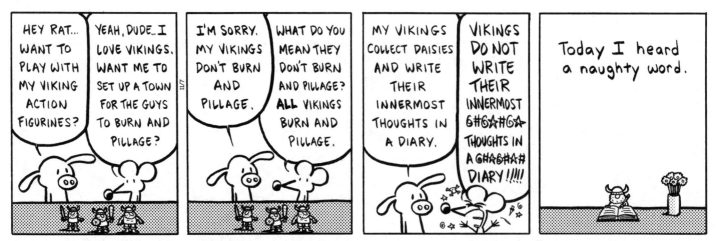

This was the first appearance of the Vikings. They were much more popular than I thought they would be, so I kept them around as semi-regular characters.

This drew an angry letter to a Florida newspaper decrying my glorification of gun violence and asking that my strip be removed from the paper. My strip stayed in the paper and nobody got shot.

I'm glad I actually used the word "spaghetti" in the last panel, because otherwise you'd have no idea what these two lumps of nothingness were supposed to be. My son asked me if they were piles of dirt. I punished him for that.

As a lawyer, I once drove off with an entire legal file sitting on the roof of my car. I had to run out into the intersection and grab all the loose papers I could. It's hard to explain to a client why there are tire tracks on his legal pleadings.

Every year, there is a county fair where I live and they have a big flower show. I went once. Sadly, I can never get that hour of my life back.

This was one of the most popular strips I've ever done. Lots of people wrote to say how much they liked the word-play. Not one person wrote to say how well I drew the anemone. That's because the anemone looks more like a pile of spaghetti than those two piles of spaghetti a couple pages back.

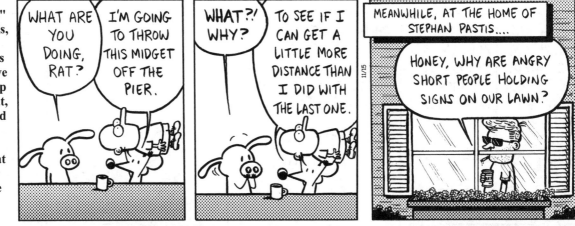

"Pearls Before Swine" creator, Stephan Pastis, is taking today off to spend time with his wife at home. Creative control of today's strip has been passed to Rat, who has promised said creator that he will avoid any and all offensive material that could trigger reader outrage. We join the strip in progress.

After this strip ran, there was an angry letter published in an Oklahoma newspaper complaining about how offensive it was to propose throwing midgets off a pier, as though this sort of thing goes on all the time in Oklahoma. He apparently missed the point that Rat was trying to write a strip that would generate complaints. Moreover, is there even a single pier in all of Oklahoma? Seeing no humor in any of this, the newspaper canceled *Pearls* a few weeks later.

This was my depiction of a columnist named Gene Weingarten, who works for the *Washington Post*. Gene's a great supporter of comics and does a weekly column that often discusses various strips. My depiction of him as a fat, unattractive man is my way of saying thanks.

My Yiayia Pana ("Yiayia" is Greek for grandmother) always used to say "fiddlesticks" whenever she was really frustrated. She died a few years ago. I really miss her.

138

I struggle with this thought all the time. I think that, in truth, we all strive to be immortal in some way. It's hard to come to terms with the notion that eventually, you'll be forgotten.

139

This one just came to me one day while driving down the highway. I saw a giant billboard touting the merits of a local crematorium and all I could think of was how much it sounded like a place that made cream.

I wrote this one while sitting on the beach staring out at the waves. If I could, I'd spend just about every day of my life at the beach.

140

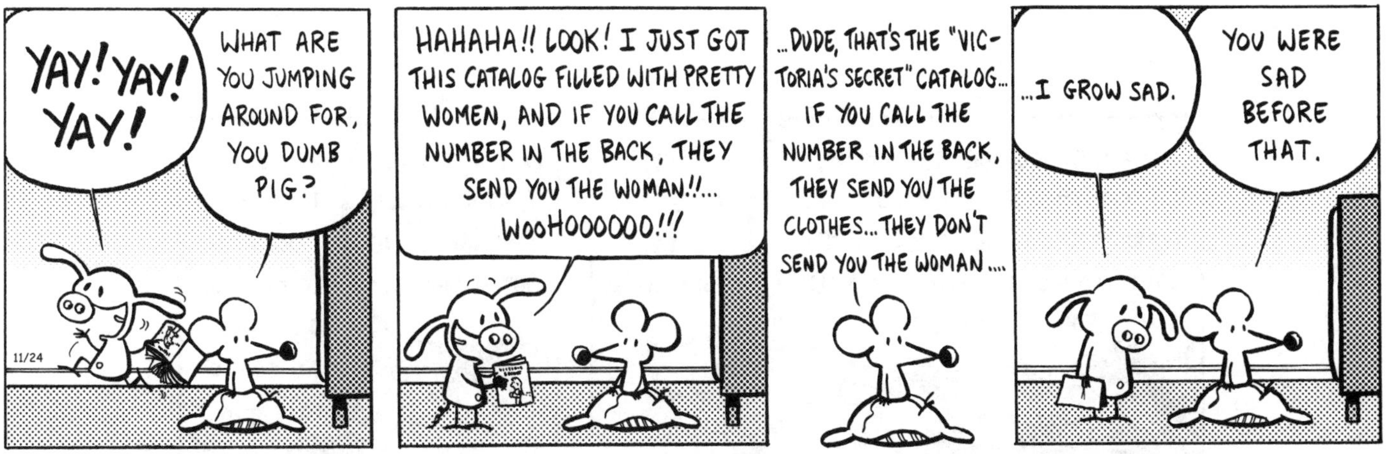
YAY! YAY! YAY!
WHAT ARE YOU JUMPING AROUND FOR, YOU DUMB PIG?
11/24
HAHAHA!! LOOK! I JUST GOT THIS CATALOG FILLED WITH PRETTY WOMEN, AND IF YOU CALL THE NUMBER IN THE BACK, THEY SEND YOU THE WOMAN!!... WOOHOOOOOO!!!
...DUDE, THAT'S THE "VICTORIA'S SECRET" CATALOG... IF YOU CALL THE NUMBER IN THE BACK, THEY SEND YOU THE CLOTHES... THEY DON'T SEND YOU THE WOMAN....
...I GROW SAD.
YOU WERE SAD BEFORE THAT.

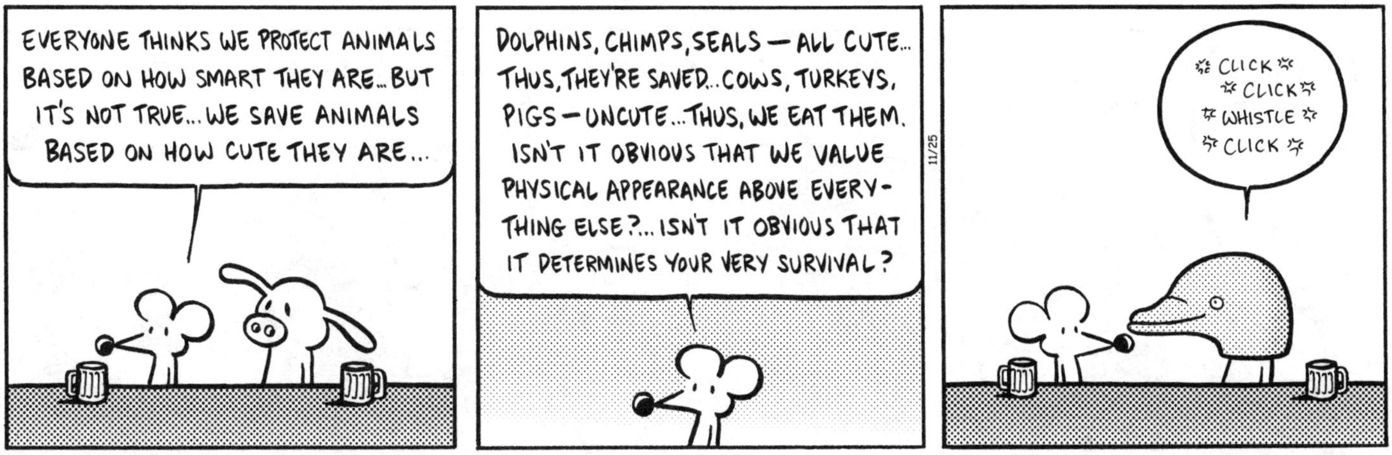
EVERYONE THINKS WE PROTECT ANIMALS BASED ON HOW SMART THEY ARE... BUT IT'S NOT TRUE... WE SAVE ANIMALS BASED ON HOW CUTE THEY ARE...
DOLPHINS, CHIMPS, SEALS — ALL CUTE... THUS, THEY'RE SAVED... COWS, TURKEYS, PIGS — UNCUTE... THUS, WE EAT THEM. ISN'T IT OBVIOUS THAT WE VALUE PHYSICAL APPEARANCE ABOVE EVERYTHING ELSE?... ISN'T IT OBVIOUS THAT IT DETERMINES YOUR VERY SURVIVAL?
11/25
CLICK CLICK WHISTLE CLICK

Originally, the strip that was supposed to run this day was a strip where Rat referred to all real estate agents as lazy and greedy. I thought the strip was a bit unfair, even for me, and so I pulled it at the last minute for this one. But for unknown reasons, some papers on the West Coast did not get the substitute in time and ran the realtor strip instead. I know this because I had a lot of angry realtors write to me, and they were all from the West Coast. You can see the original realtor strip in the "Not Ready for Prime Time Comic Strips" section of this book.

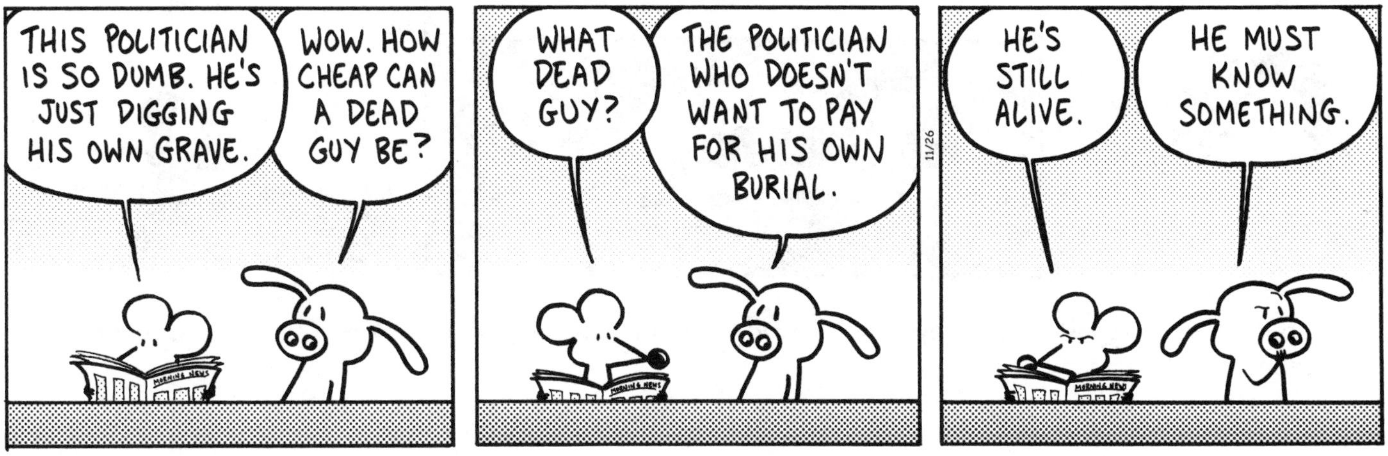
THIS POLITICIAN IS SO DUMB. HE'S JUST DIGGING HIS OWN GRAVE.
WOW. HOW CHEAP CAN A DEAD GUY BE?
WHAT DEAD GUY?
THE POLITICIAN WHO DOESN'T WANT TO PAY FOR HIS OWN BURIAL.
11/26
HE'S STILL ALIVE.
HE MUST KNOW SOMETHING.

This strip idea was suggested to me by the aforesaid Gene Weingarten, who wanted to see what would happen if the zebra tried to eat the crocs.

I actually read a book of Robert Frost poems last year. I only understood about three of them, but that's three more than I've ever understood in any other poetry book.

I think Scott Adams mentioned that he liked this strip in his blog. I always love it when I get a compliment from Scott.

A rare over-the-shoulder perspective in that third panel. I must have been feeling cocky that day.

After this ran, I got a bunch of e-mail from various people who attended a church in Minnesota asking me if I was referring to *their* Father Nick, who had just died. They thought it was a tribute. Unfortunately, I had no idea who they were talking about.

Somebody wrote to me after this ran and asked if Pig was supposed to represent New Orleans in the wake of Hurricane Katrina. I didn't intend that, but I thought it was a pretty interesting observation.

Love never seems to work out well in my strip.

146

One of the great things about doing a comic strip is that I can take anything that annoys me and have Rat vent my frustration.

This is an old strip that I decided to run probably two years after it was drawn. I just didn't think it was that strong of a strip so I kept putting off its publication.

Sometimes when I do strips like this that mention specific stores, I worry about whether the store is simply regional (i.e., that people on the East Coast might not know what "Safeway" is). For this reason, I have to make sure the reader can get the joke whether or not they've ever heard of the store.

Someone gave one of these Harmony Care Bears to my daughter. As befits his name, I believe his job is to promote love and understanding between different people. Naturally, my first thought was to send him to Iraq.

This was the debut of the killer whale, a character I really liked. I think I drew these after a visit to Sea World in San Diego.

The killer whale holds the distinction of being the *Pearls* character that requires the most ink.

This is another old strip I held off publishing for quite a while, mostly because of the drug reference. I finally buried it on this Saturday near Christmas, secretly hoping that everyone would be out shopping instead of reading the newspaper.

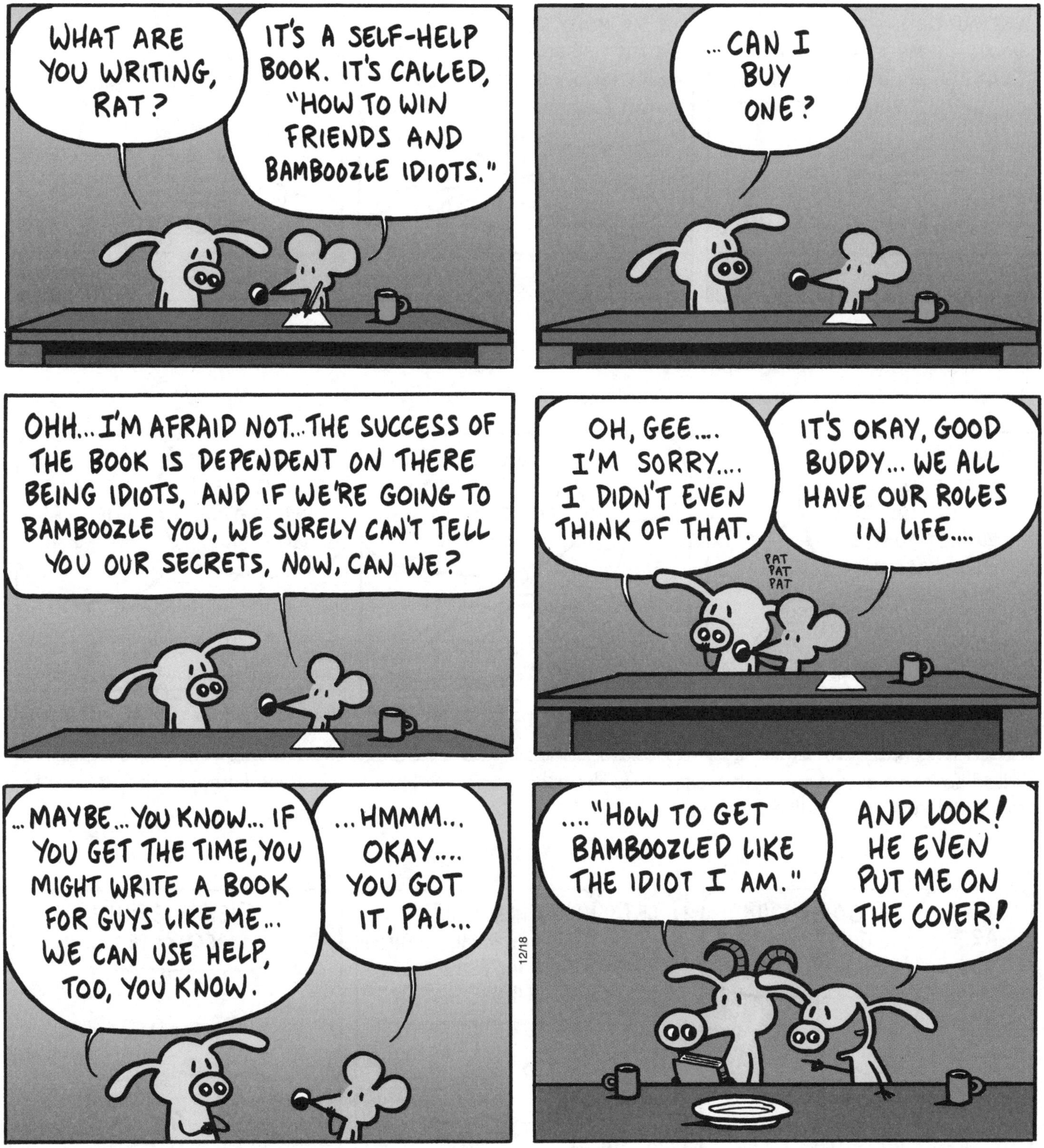
WHAT ARE YOU WRITING, RAT?
IT'S A SELF-HELP BOOK. IT'S CALLED, "HOW TO WIN FRIENDS AND BAMBOOZLE IDIOTS."
...CAN I BUY ONE?
OHH... I'M AFRAID NOT... THE SUCCESS OF THE BOOK IS DEPENDENT ON THERE BEING IDIOTS, AND IF WE'RE GOING TO BAMBOOZLE YOU, WE SURELY CAN'T TELL YOU OUR SECRETS, NOW, CAN WE?
OH, GEE.... I'M SORRY.... I DIDN'T EVEN THINK OF THAT.
PAT PAT PAT
IT'S OKAY, GOOD BUDDY... WE ALL HAVE OUR ROLES IN LIFE....
...MAYBE... YOU KNOW... IF YOU GET THE TIME, YOU MIGHT WRITE A BOOK FOR GUYS LIKE ME... WE CAN USE HELP, TOO, YOU KNOW.
...HMMM... OKAY.... YOU GOT IT, PAL...
12/18
...."HOW TO GET BAMBOOZLED LIKE THE IDIOT I AM."
AND LOOK! HE EVEN PUT ME ON THE COVER!

It's odd how so many of my "curb scene" strips show that same can littering the street. Perhaps I should learn to draw a different piece of litter.

I like to sometimes read people their horoscopes, wait for them to say, "Oh my God, that's totally my life," and then announce to them I was reading the horoscope of a different sign.

This and "To be or not to be" are the only two Shakespeare quotes I know. But I include them in the strip to make me look smart.

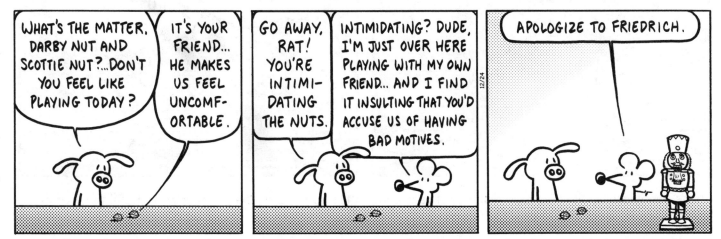

Originally, in that second panel, Pig was saying, "You're intimidating my nuts," but that sounded too much like a potential body part, so I had to change it to "the" nuts. Also, I named these two nuts after Darby Conley and Scott Adams. It made me laugh to name a potential body part after them.

That's one wickedly detailed tape dispenser I've drawn on the floor there. The good news is that if this was an outdoor scene, it could also pass for a snail.

I didn't like this series, so I held on to it for a couple years and then finally buried it in the week after Christmas, hoping again that no one was reading the paper. As it turned out, it was fairly popular. When I look back on it now, I think I was more afraid than anything because I was using the word "damn" in the Tuesday strip (12/27) and "sucks" in the Thursday strip (12/29), and both of those can cause problems.

As expected, I did see some angry letters to editors after this one ran.

Another thing that worried me about this week was whether or not the text would be understandable. This was the one I was the most worried about. As it turned out, no one complained. Perhaps they were too busy complaining about the word "damn" the day before.

I never got to meet Johnny Hart.

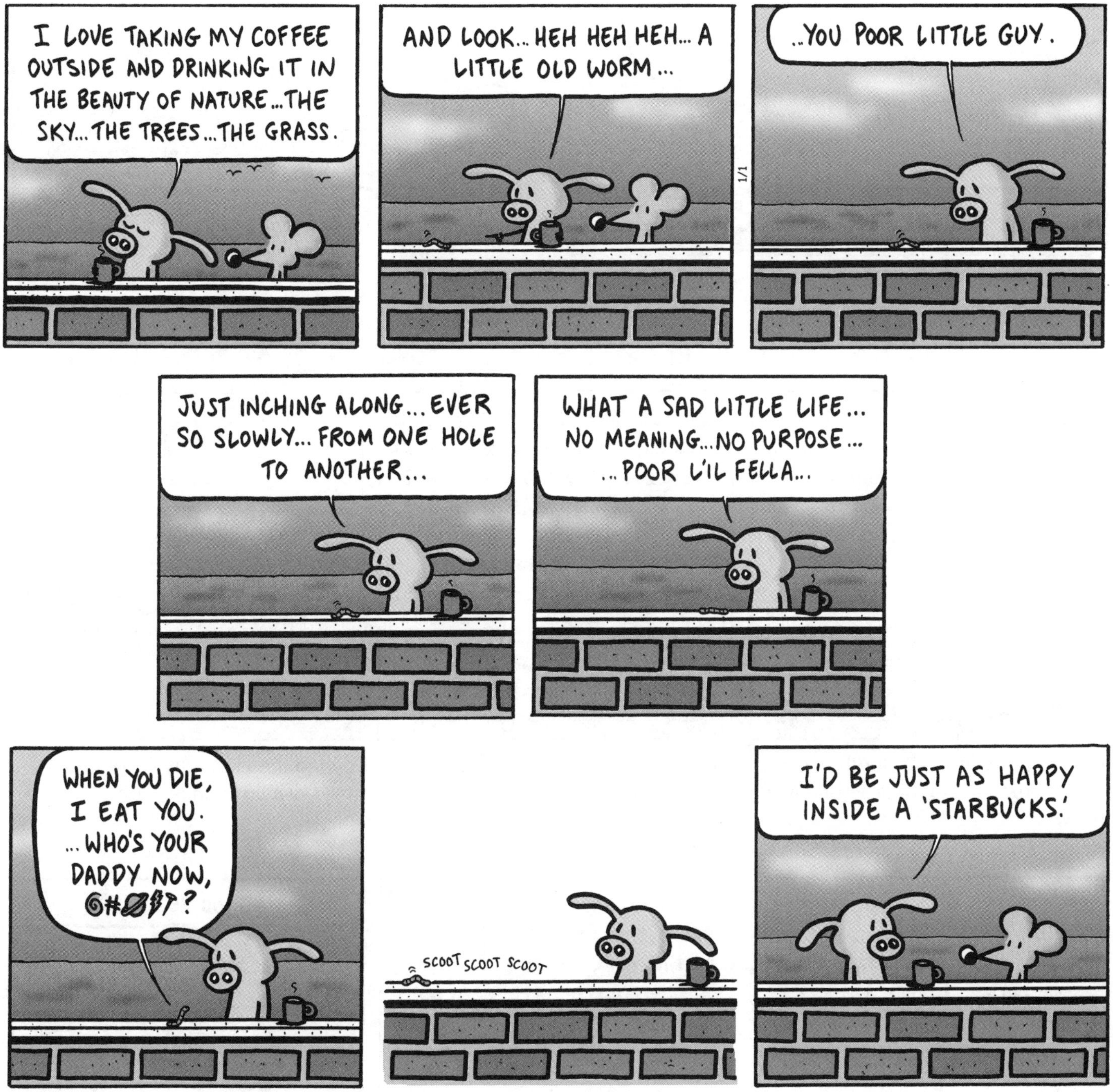
I LOVE TAKING MY COFFEE OUTSIDE AND DRINKING IT IN THE BEAUTY OF NATURE...THE SKY...THE TREES...THE GRASS.
AND LOOK... HEH HEH HEH... A LITTLE OLD WORM...
..YOU POOR LITTLE GUY.
JUST INCHING ALONG... EVER SO SLOWLY... FROM ONE HOLE TO ANOTHER...
WHAT A SAD LITTLE LIFE... NO MEANING...NO PURPOSE... ...POOR L'IL FELLA...
WHEN YOU DIE, I EAT YOU. ...WHO'S YOUR DADDY NOW, #?
SCOOT SCOOT SCOOT
I'D BE JUST AS HAPPY INSIDE A 'STARBUCKS.'

I think I was influenced by the *Calvin and Hobbes* snowman gags here.

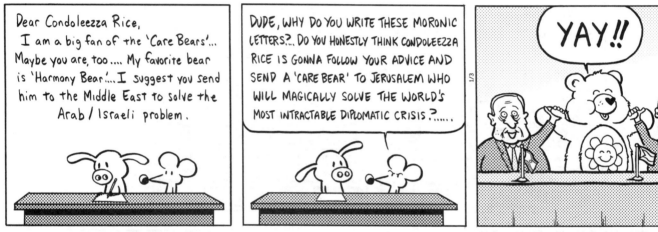

If there's anything harder than drawing the Harmony Care Bear for me, it's drawing the Harmony Care Bear sitting next to Ariel Sharon and Mahmoud Abbas. It's days like this that make me wish cartooning didn't involve drawing.

HEY THERE, RAT... LISTEN, I HAVE TO BRING THE DESSERT FOR A POTLUCK ENGAGEMENT PARTY MY FRIENDS ARE HAVING AND I THOUGHT I COULD BRING SOME OF YOUR GINGERBREAD MEN.

HMMMM... I THINK I HAVE SOMETHING WITH A MAN AND WIFE THEME... AH, YES, HERE IT IS... I EVEN GAVE IT A NICE TITLE...

OH, YEAH?... WHAT IS IT?

"BOB AND TERRY HAVE THEIR DIFFERENCES."

...YOU KNOW, MAYBE I'LL JUST PICK UP SOMETHING AT THE STORE.

PEOPLE WITH EDIBLE HEADS REALLY SHOULDN'T FIGHT.

WHAT ARE YOU FILLING OUT, RAT?

IT'S A JOB QUESTIONNAIRE... IT MATCHES YOU WITH YOUR PERFECT CAREER... RIGHT NOW, IT LOOKS LIKE I GOT 'PROFESSIONAL CRITIC' WRITTEN ALL OVER ME.

WHAT'S A 'PROFESSIONAL CRITIC'?

IT SAYS..."SOMEONE WHO SO LACKS THE NECESSARY SKILL TO ENTER A GIVEN PROFESSION THAT THEY CHOOSE INSTEAD TO SIT IN JUDGMENT OF IT... SEE, ALSO, 'BITTER BETTY.'"

SOMEONE PAYS YOU TO BE BITTER?

THE BITTERER THE BETTERER.

It really is strange to me that some people get paid to offer their opinion on something they couldn't hope to do themselves. My theory is that if you really know so much about it, you should be able to do it yourself. Otherwise, how much do you really understand?

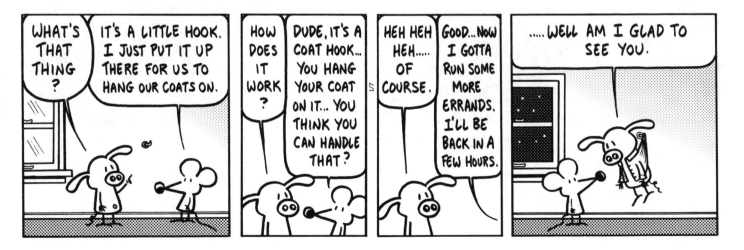

WHAT'S THAT THING?

IT'S A LITTLE HOOK. I JUST PUT IT UP THERE FOR US TO HANG OUR COATS ON.

HOW DOES IT WORK?

DUDE, IT'S A COAT HOOK... YOU HANG YOUR COAT ON IT... YOU THINK YOU CAN HANDLE THAT?

HEH HEH HEH..... OF COURSE.

GOOD...NOW I GOTTA RUN SOME MORE ERRANDS. I'LL BE BACK IN A FEW HOURS.

.....WELL AM I GLAD TO SEE YOU.

My one and only attempt at drawing Bill Gates. I was hoping he would see it and offer a million dollars for the original. He did not.

I'm very proud of that shower cap. It is the best-drawn shower cap to ever appear in my comic strip.

When I was a little kid, I loved to watch John McEnroe lose his temper during matches. Tennis needs more of that nowadays. That and fistfights. I'd watch tennis if I thought a fistfight might break out.

Hey, I just noticed a mistake in this one. I forgot to add the dot shading to that bush in the first panel. I shall fire my editor.

I actually live in the wine country here in Northern California. And just like that old guy in the third panel, I have terrible allergies. I spend all of May sneezing.

I got this idea while staring at two little garden gnomes we have on the back patio. I'm not sure where the gnomes came from. I think my wife bought them. I never buy anything. I never shop. I am almost entirely worthless in the overall household structure.

I eat a lot of uncooked broccoli. I like broccoli. That's the sort of commentary that makes the purchase of this book worthwhile.

There's that can in the street again. But this time I have gone all out and drawn *additional* pieces of litter. Wow. Now that's impressive.

That hubcap in the last panel took me a half hour to draw. Please take a moment to appreciate it.

This is one of my own pet peeves, so I thought I'd make fun of people who do it. Why do people feel compelled to e-mail you any little thing they find of any interest? I've never understood that. Thank God for the "report SPAM" button on AOL.

In the original of this strip, the punchline was "This place sucks." But I was not allowed to use the word "sucks." If I could lobby for the use of just one additional word on the comics page, it would be "sucks."

By this day, I was getting very tired of drawing these same five puffy-lipped fellows.

Nowadays, when I draw an open mouth like the one in the second panel, I show the inside of it (i.e., I fill the mouth in with black and put a tongue in it). I think it looks better that way. So now, when I look back at the mouths I used to draw, I think they look sort of odd.

Not one taxicab driver complained about this comic. That's reason enough for me to like all taxicab drivers.

I get asked sometimes why I don't write a blog. I'm not sure, really. I know Scott Adams does it and likes it. Maybe one day.

Personally, this is one of my favorite strips. Every time I see the last panel, I laugh. It just seems so wildly inappropriate to poke a body like that at a funeral.

I've been lucky enough to go to Tokyo a couple of times. I loved it. And man, are they crazy about cartoon characters.

Is anyone on an internet message board really who they say they are?

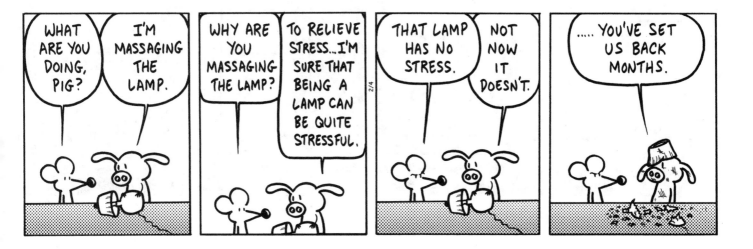

171

"Bradbury" is the street I used to live on as a kid.

The anemone turned out to be a very popular character. I just liked the idea of someone as sweet as Pig having a mortal enemy.

If you look in that second panel, there's a tiny framed picture of an ocean, which is where sea anemones come from. This is called foreshadowing. I am one clever fellow.

A tiny bit of political commentary in that first panel. I can get away with it if it's not the focus of the strip.

The third, fourth, and fifth panels of this comic offer a wonderful example of why I try not to draw cars in my comic. Drawing cars = Kiss of Death for Stephan.

I gave the whale the same lowercase speech as the other major predator in the strip, the crocodiles.

That fourth panel is the first time I ever tried to draw a head-on view of one of the crocs. It still looks kind of funny to me, so I rarely try it.

These Valentine's Day strips ran shortly after my strip first started running in the *Arizona Republic*, the largest newspaper in Arizona, and the only newspaper my dad reads. After the series ran, my dad called me and asked, "Do you really have to kill so many things?"

That's me at the top of the pile in the last panel.

I've never even seen *Ellen*, but I assume it's a show a Viking wouldn't typically watch.

DEAR LIONS,
   YOUR KILLING OF MY FELLOW ZEBRAS HAS INCREASED AS OF LATE...AFTER A GREAT DEAL OF THOUGHT, I BELIEVE I'VE DISCOVERED THE SOURCE OF YOUR HOSTILITY...

PSYCHOLOGISTS BELIEVE THAT AN INDIVIDUAL WHO LACKS A CREATIVE OUTLET IS MORE LIKELY TO COMMIT A VIOLENT ACT....YOU, THE LIONS, HAVE NO CREATIVE OUTLET.

TO RECTIFY THE PROBLEM, I SUGGEST YOU TAKE A FEW MOMENTS EACH DAY TO COMPOSE A POEM OR TWO... IT DOESN'T HAVE TO BE PARTICULARLY GOOD OR ARTFUL...THE POINT IS REALLY JUST TO GET YOUR THOUGHTS DOWN ON PAPER.

I BELIEVE THE EFFECTS OF THIS WILL BE IMMEDIATE AND YOUR IMPULSE TO KILL WILL BE ERADICATED...GO AHEAD.. GIVE IT A TRY!

Roses is red.
Violets is blue.
Me me me
Kill you you you.

...SIGH.

This strip harkens back to the early days of the strip when Zebra wrote frequent letters to his predators. Now, with predators like the crocs entrenched right next door to Zebra, I don't do this letter-writing gag as much.

I thought this was a funny one. I seem to like my strip better when it's at its darkest.

The Vikings have turned out to be pretty popular characters.

Panel Two: Best paper bag I've ever drawn.

I had to actually stare at my little Honda Accord while drawing this strip in order to learn how to draw the inside of a car. One would think I would know what the inside of my car looks like, given that I've owned it for fourteen years, but one would be wrong.

That second panel offers a good summary of Pig's life view.

This was a very popular strip, so much so that I made the last panel the cover of the 2008 *Pearls* Day-to-Day Calendar.

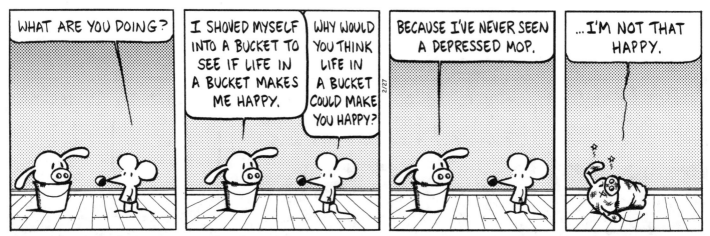

The week I drew this strip we got hardwood floors installed in our house. Easily influenced, I added the hardwood floor to this particular strip. It was a lot cheaper to draw it in the strip than it was to install it in the house.

Originally, the croc in the toilet was saying, "Ahhhhhhh," as in, "This is so relaxing." But after I drew it, and saw it in context of the toilet, it made it look like the croc was relieving himself. So I deleted the "Ahhhhhhh." That saved at least 200 uptight people a lot of time they would otherwise have spent writing to their newspaper editor that day.

A number of people wrote me to tell me that killer whales do not eat krill. This is true. They also don't drive little cars to McDonald's.

I thought I was going to get into a lot of trouble for this modified version of the Sermon on the Mount, but hardly anyone complained. I'm so often surprised at what does and does not elicit complaints.

I actually saw this clip on one of those nature shows. The killer whale just leaps onto the beach and grabs this little seal. Makes you think twice about volunteering to be kissed by Shamu the next time you're at Sea World.

Rat is constantly trying to think up ways to shut out the world.

I believe this is the first time I ever drew Rat from the side view. I'm still not sure I got it quite right.

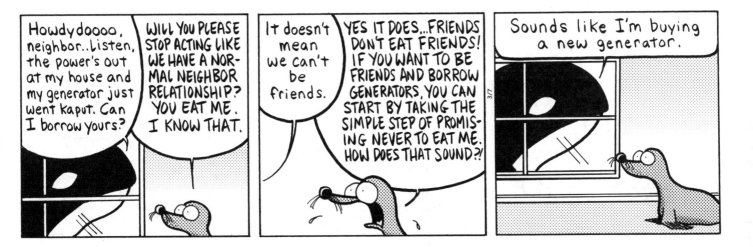

I think I wrote these "Dog O' Abject Despondency" strips after having watched too much cable news. That can really depress a guy.

This strip and the one after it were much more popular than I thought they'd be, proving once again that I have almost no idea how strips will be received.

I am not a huge Celine Dion fan. You may have guessed that from this strip.

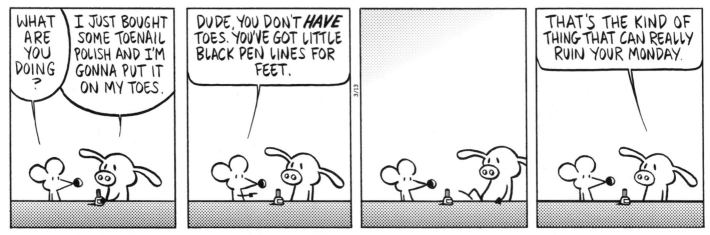

I like to play around with the characters' awareness that they are just ink drawings.

I'm quite proud of that hole. It looks almost like a hole.

Apathy is the true key to happiness.

Note the subtle detail of the stars in the sky. It's that kind of detail that makes me an artistic master.

Ohhh, man. This series drew way more complaints than I thought it would. Something about mixing kids and alcohol and having Rat babysit while drunk just threw some uptight readers over the edge. Many of them responded like I had actually endangered real kids, making no allowance for the fact that the *Baby Blues* kids are made of ink. The irony of it was that the creators of *Baby Blues*, Jerry Scott and Rick Kirkman, had seen the entire series and thought it was funny.

One very angry female reader wrote to *both* Rick Kirkman and me, upset at me for drawing these strips and upset at him for "letting" his characters be used like this. Rick made the mistake of defending me, and she got even angrier. Defending me against uptight comic strip readers is never a good idea.

Just for fun, I put a *Pearls Before Swine* shirt on the little girl, Zoe.

Readers who were mad about the first few strips in this series just about blew a gasket when they saw this strip. Not only had I endangered the *Baby Blues* kids, but I had now killed the kid from *Zits*. My theory is that if you're gonna make people mad, you might as well get your money's worth.

For being such great sports, I named these two crocs after Jerry Scott and Rick Kirkman.

The funniest part of this whole *Baby Blues* series was that in the next Monday's *Baby Blues* strip, Rick drew a beat-up crocodile on the floor of the kids' living room, proving to everyone that Rick and Jerry knew about this in advance. I think that quieted down some of the outrage toward me.

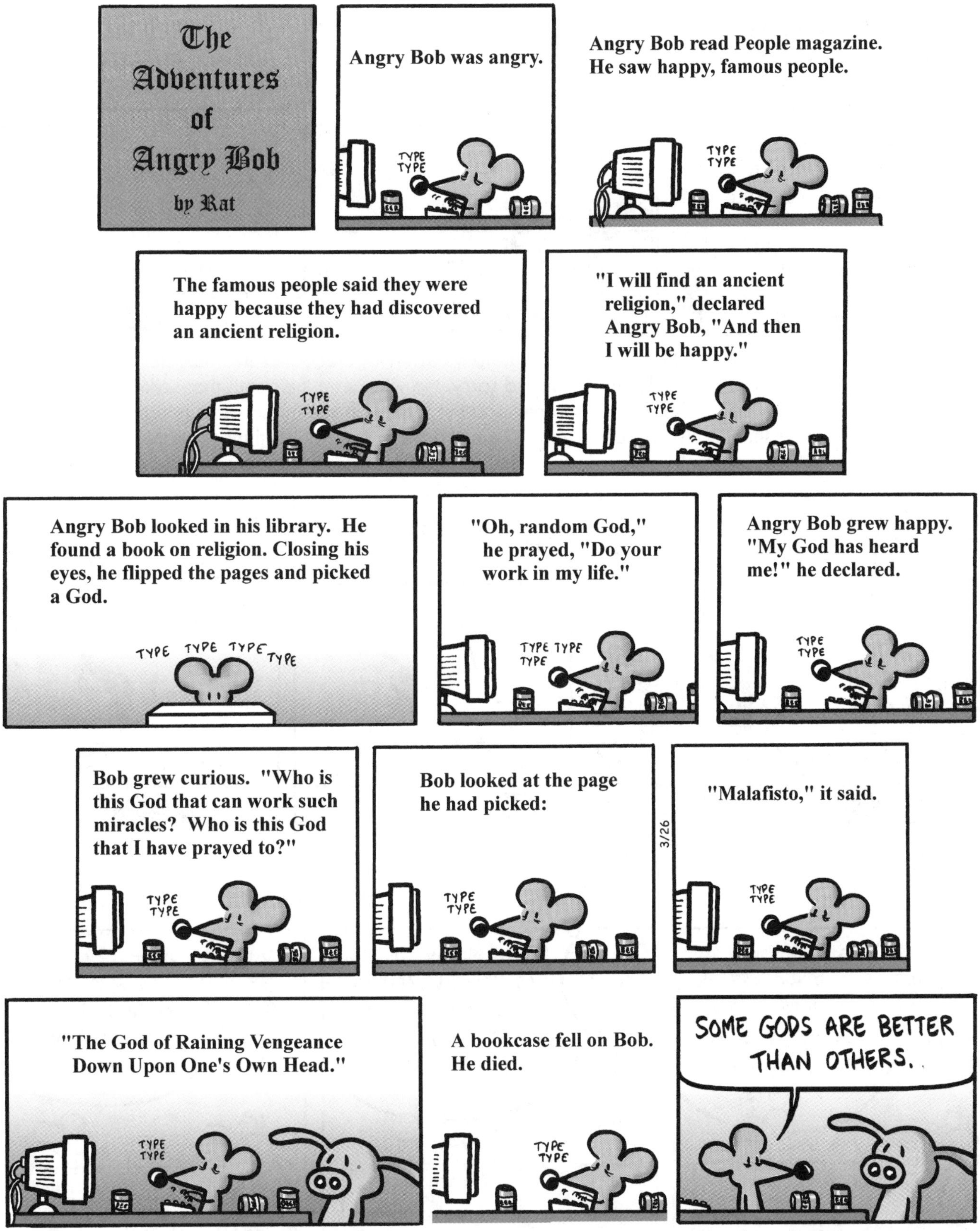
The Adventures of Angry Bob
by Rat
Angry Bob was angry.
TYPE TYPE
Angry Bob read People magazine. He saw happy, famous people.
TYPE TYPE
The famous people said they were happy because they had discovered an ancient religion.
TYPE TYPE
"I will find an ancient religion," declared Angry Bob, "And then I will be happy."
TYPE TYPE
Angry Bob looked in his library. He found a book on religion. Closing his eyes, he flipped the pages and picked a God.
TYPE TYPE TYPE TYPE
"Oh, random God," he prayed, "Do your work in my life."
TYPE TYPE TYPE
Angry Bob grew happy. "My God has heard me!" he declared.
TYPE TYPE
Bob grew curious. "Who is this God that can work such miracles? Who is this God that I have prayed to?"
TYPE TYPE
Bob looked at the page he had picked:
3/26
TYPE TYPE
"Malafisto," it said.
TYPE TYPE
"The God of Raining Vengeance Down Upon One's Own Head."
TYPE TYPE
A bookcase fell on Bob. He died.
TYPE TYPE
SOME GODS ARE BETTER THAN OTHERS.

It's been established in the strip that the Zeeba Zeeba Eata fraternity of crocodiles live next door to Zebra. However, there is also this family of crocodiles (the husband Larry, the wife, and their son) that seem to live next door to Zebra as well. I've never established if the fraternity and the family all live in the same house or not. As far as I'm concerned, the whole situation is very confusing. If I were a better cartoonist, things like this wouldn't happen.

Predictably, Rat's reaction angered a few people.

My wife, Staci, always writes our thank-you cards. But I don't think she calls anyone "el cheapo." Of course, I wouldn't know that because I never actually read them. It's revelations like this that could really cause my popularity to decline.

195

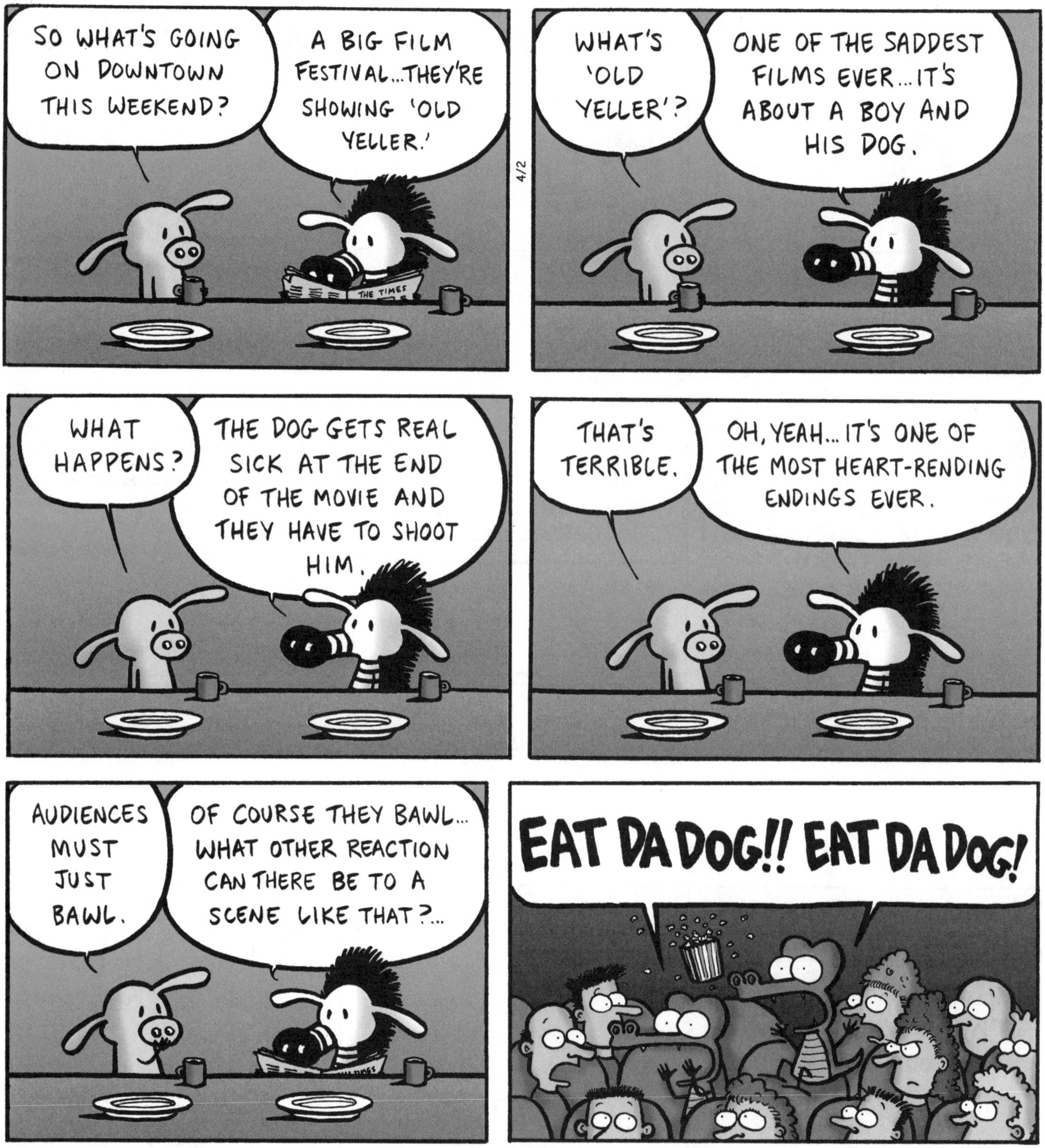
SO WHAT'S GOING ON DOWNTOWN THIS WEEKEND?
A BIG FILM FESTIVAL...THEY'RE SHOWING 'OLD YELLER.'
THE TIMES
4/2
WHAT'S 'OLD YELLER'?
ONE OF THE SADDEST FILMS EVER...IT'S ABOUT A BOY AND HIS DOG.
WHAT HAPPENS?
THE DOG GETS REAL SICK AT THE END OF THE MOVIE AND THEY HAVE TO SHOOT HIM.
THAT'S TERRIBLE.
OH, YEAH... IT'S ONE OF THE MOST HEART-RENDING ENDINGS EVER.
AUDIENCES MUST JUST BAWL.
OF COURSE THEY BAWL... WHAT OTHER REACTION CAN THERE BE TO A SCENE LIKE THAT?...
EAT DA DOG!! EAT DA DOG!

I like to bring Farina back from time to time. But every time I do, I always have to reintroduce who she is for newspaper readers who may be new to the strip.

I like strips like this because they show that Rat does have a heart, black though it may be. Sort of helps to round out his character.

197

I'm often asked why the crocs have never tried to eat Pig. I don't have a good answer for that. Once again, if I were a better cartoonist, this sort of thing wouldn't happen.

I really liked the whale/seal strips, but not a lot of other people seemed to share my view. I don't know why he didn't catch on like the crocs did.

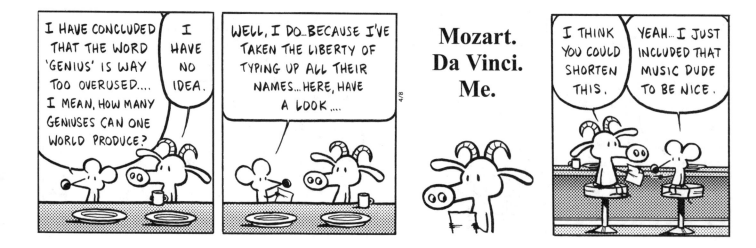

198

Every now and then, I still feel compelled to throw in a bad pun.

For those who don't yet know, Scott Adams launched my career in December 2000 when he told all of his readers that he liked my strip and that they should go read it. I will forever owe him for that.

I don't know why, but it amuses me that the one girl Rat gives his heart to really gets around.

A rare appearance by my wife Staci in the strip. I guess she was taking a break from writing all those thank-you cards.

201

This marked the introduction of Danny Donkey, a character who turned out to be quite popular with readers. He resulted from a day of writing where I purposely tried to just block everything out of my head (including my own regular characters). Now you can see what occupies the dark recesses of my mind.

A few weeks before these strips appeared, Darby Conley (*Get Fuzzy*) and I came up with the strange idea of having him rip off almost this entire week's worth of *Pearls Before Swine* strips. What he did was to draw himself in his own comic accidentally receiving a week's worth of *Pearls* strips from our common syndicate, United Feature Syndicate. Then, for the next four days of *Get Fuzzy*, Darby simply published the four *Pearls* strips you see below (beginning with the hammer strip and ending with the plate strip) with Bucky and Satchel crudely pasted over my characters. I thought it was a lot of fun, but for *Get Fuzzy* readers who had never seen my strip before, it must have been extremely confusing (especially when they saw Satchel being attacked by tiny little crocodiles with hammers). The funniest part for me was the readers who e-mailed me to see if I knew that some jerk was ripping me off.

203

Originally, in the second panel of this strip, the croc was reading straight out of the Bible, which then gets knocked out of his hand. But I knew that was guaranteed to make a lot of people very angry, so I toned it down to what you see here. The original of this strip can be seen in the "Not Ready for Prime Time Comic Strips" section of this book.

Like many people, I absolutely cannot stand someone talking loudly into a cell phone in a restaurant. I'm not sure why it's any different than the same person talking loudly to someone who's actually sitting with him in his booth, but it sure seems more obnoxious.

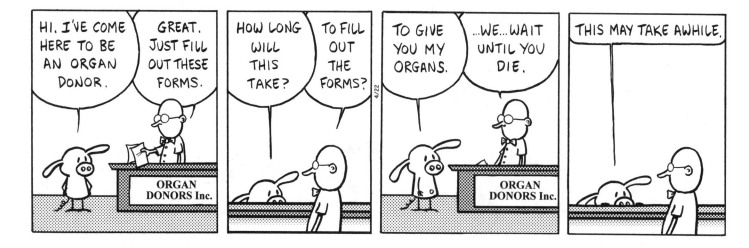

I think I must have gotten all those smiley faces and rainbows from the comic strip *Rose is Rose*.

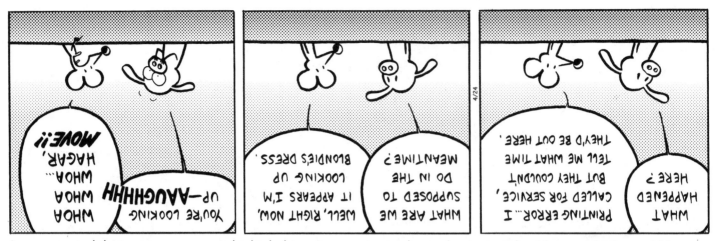

I was worried that some papers might think this strip was a mistake and print it right side up, which would have ruined everything, but I didn't hear of that happening. What I did hear was feedback from readers who thought the strip was very funny because in their paper *Pearls* actually DID appear below the comic strip *Blondie*.

Had I not taken high school geometry, I might not have known the meaning of the word "perpendicular." So stay in school, kids.

206

A few weeks after these U.P.S. strips appeared, the U.P.S. driver who delivers to our house found out who I was and asked my wife if the strips were based on a female driver who sometimes delivers packages in our area. Given that I never answer the door and thus have never actually seen any of our U.P.S. drivers, my wife had to tell him no.

207

I like having Rat use outdated expressions, like "hecka." It makes his arrogance about his own stature in life all the more ridiculous.

"Stromoski" was named after Rick Stromoski, the creator of the comic strip *Soup to Nutz* and the former president of the National Cartoonists Society. Rick responded to this strip by introducing a character into his strip named "Stephan" whose one defining characteristic was that he had a gigantically oversized head.

I thought this was the funniest of all the whale strips.

I'm quite proud of my Barbara Bush caricature.

This unfortunate strip ran in May 2006. As everyone knows, Steve Irwin died four months later, in September 2006.

I liked the way the crocs looked in these monk robes.

This letter resulted in what I thought was one of the funniest complaint letters ever published in a newspaper about *Pearls*. The writer called it "disgusting" and "crude" that I would mention a nun having an enema with Eminem. I'm not sure whether it was the enema or Eminem that pushed her over the edge, but clearly the combination of the two was too much for her. She termed the strip a "slap in the face" to her "three aunts in the convent" and to the nuns that had given her children "an excellent education." The funny part for me was that the only reason the word "nun" was in there at all was that I needed it for the phrase "a nun and me" (which is meant to sound like "anemone").

212

I'm proud of my introducing the word "skzzinkss" into the lexicon of comics. Roughly translated, it means, "the sound of one getting up."

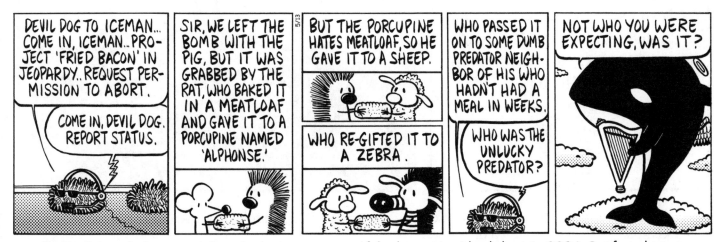

I really liked the whale strips. I thought they were some of the best strips I had done in 2006. But for whatever reason, they just didn't seem to catch on with most readers. Thus, I took the rare step of killing one of my regular characters. The funny part was that as soon as he died, all these fans of the whale seemed to come out of the woodwork, each asking for him to be brought back. But it was too late. The poor guy was a goner.

213

The chained croc's line in the last panel is taken from Muhammad Ali. Shortly after beating Sonny Liston, he yelled to reporters, "I'm a baaaad man."

The "Jason" I drew here is a friend of mine. This is the kind of thing I do for friends.

This image of Pig doing the hula seemed to be pretty popular with readers.

I frequently get e-mails telling me I should quit smoking. But as I've said before, I don't smoke. I also get e-mails telling me that I glamorize smoking by drawing it in the strip. But my intention is the exact opposite. I do it to make me look like more of a degenerate loser. It's sort of a "Hey kids, don't end up like this" message.

This strip is sort of a throwback to the early days of *Pearls* when most of my strips were simply three panels of Rat and Pig talking to each other. There's still a fair number of those, but not as many as there once were.

Pig's experience at the gym counter came straight out of my own life. But in addition to doing this to the woman at the gym counter, I also do it every time I'm about to board a flight. The airline employee I hand my ticket to says, "Have a nice flight," and I say, "You too," even though *they're* not flying anywhere. It always makes me feel like a big fat idiot.

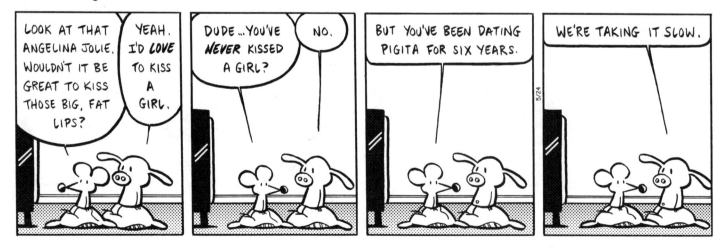

When I was in law school, I had to take a class on "torts," which is basically when someone violates a civil duty owed to someone else. But every time the professor mentioned the word "duty," the guy next to me would purposely misinterpret the word as "doody," as in something you'd leave behind in the toilet. Sometimes he would even draw pictures of this little doody and pass them to me. Even though I was supposed to be a mature law school student, it made me laugh so hard that I would sometimes have to leave the class.

Farina really does get around. At least Ziggy would be around the right height for her.

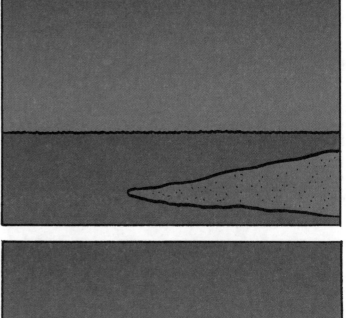

5/28

**A moment of silence
in honor of the American
men and women killed
in Iraq and Afghanistan.**

Memorial Day, 2006

I don't typically do serious strips like this, but I frequently hear from American soldiers in Iraq and Afghanistan and wanted them to know I was thinking about them and the sacrifices that they and their fellow soldiers were making. Even though the reaction to the strip was largely positive, the strip also drew complaints from people who were angry that I was singling out these specific wars. Their argument was that Memorial Day was meant to honor fallen soldiers from *all* of the American wars, and that to single out the wars in Afghanistan and Iraq could only be interpreted as a political statement. I didn't see it that way.

Originally, Rat was saying, "My butt itches," but I changed it to "rear end." Believe it or not, "butt" is one of those iffy words that can sometimes generate complaints. The comics page is probably the only place in all of American entertainment where the word "butt" is considered edgy.

Pearls doesn't yet run in Alaska, which is why I can make jokes like this.

When I draw strips like this one, I draw them with my left hand.

This strip generated an absolutely irate e-mail from a woman demanding that I show more respect toward Gloria Steinem. I think the moment a cartoonist becomes "respectful" is the moment his career begins to end.

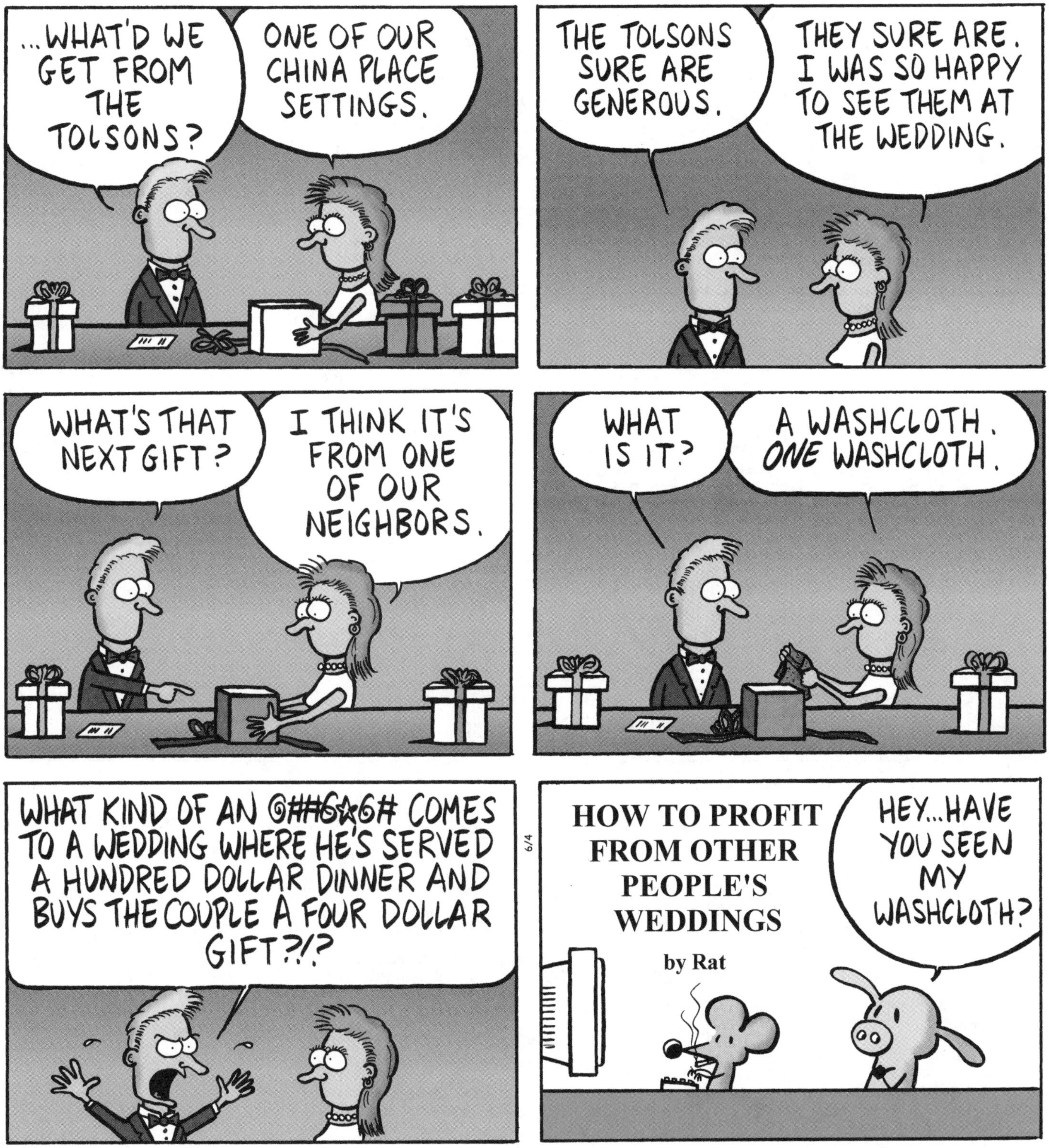
...WHAT'D WE GET FROM THE TOLSONS?
ONE OF OUR CHINA PLACE SETTINGS.
THE TOLSONS SURE ARE GENEROUS.
THEY SURE ARE. I WAS SO HAPPY TO SEE THEM AT THE WEDDING.
WHAT'S THAT NEXT GIFT?
I THINK IT'S FROM ONE OF OUR NEIGHBORS.
WHAT IS IT?
A WASHCLOTH. *ONE* WASHCLOTH.
WHAT KIND OF AN @##@☆@# COMES TO A WEDDING WHERE HE'S SERVED A HUNDRED DOLLAR DINNER AND BUYS THE COUPLE A FOUR DOLLAR GIFT?!?
6/4
HOW TO PROFIT FROM OTHER PEOPLE'S WEDDINGS
by Rat
HEY...HAVE YOU SEEN MY WASHCLOTH?

Please take a moment to really appreciate that open door in the first panel, because it took me about a half hour to draw.

I have reached the conclusion that *Kill Bill* really is the greatest film I have ever seen. The whole thing is just mesmerizing in its originality.

For the record, I have never watched *Steel Magnolias*, but I hear someone dies.

Lawrence of Arabia is also one of my favorite movies.

225

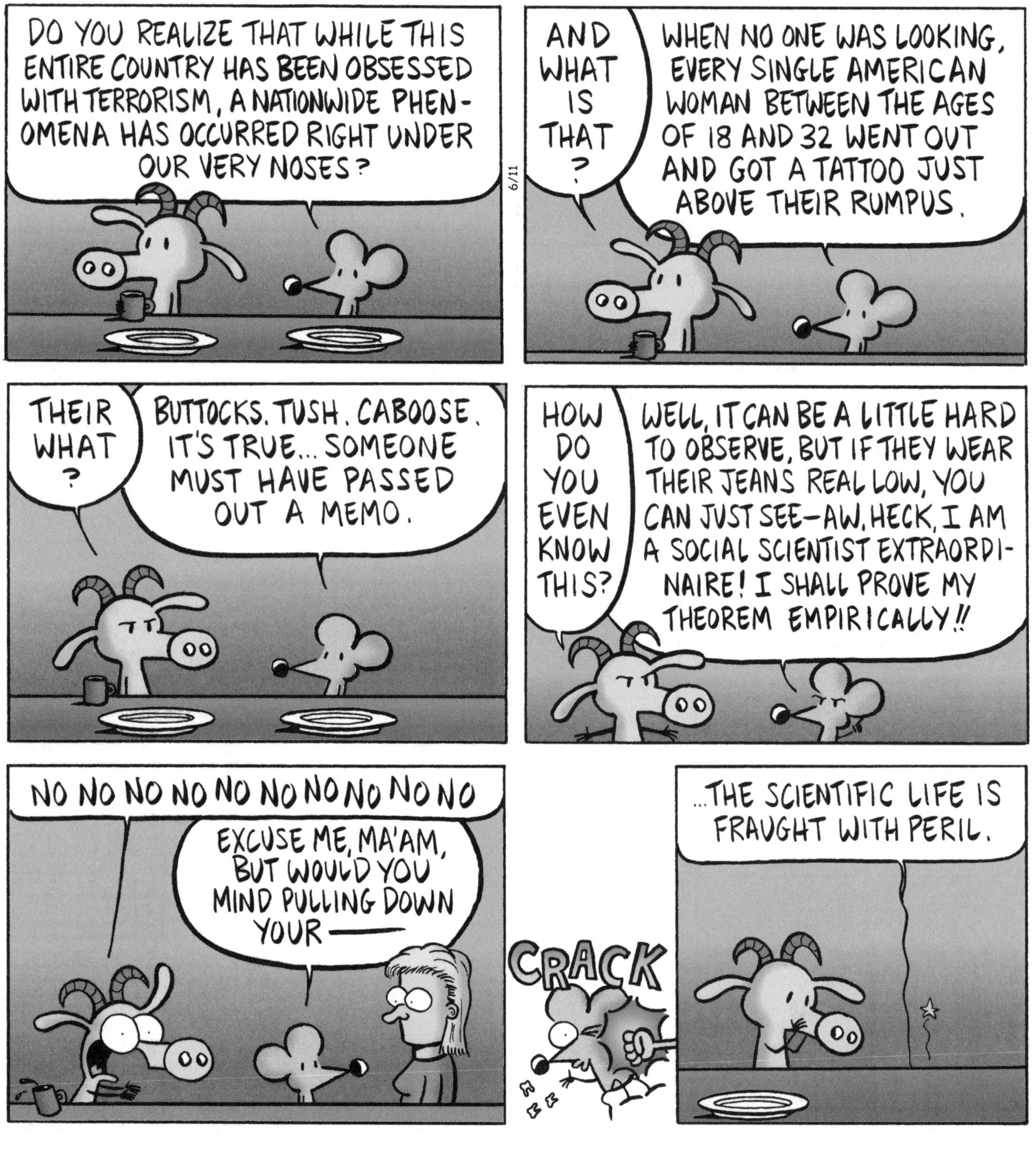
DO YOU REALIZE THAT WHILE THIS ENTIRE COUNTRY HAS BEEN OBSESSED WITH TERRORISM, A NATIONWIDE PHENOMENA HAS OCCURRED RIGHT UNDER OUR VERY NOSES?
6/11
AND WHAT IS THAT?
WHEN NO ONE WAS LOOKING, EVERY SINGLE AMERICAN WOMAN BETWEEN THE AGES OF 18 AND 32 WENT OUT AND GOT A TATTOO JUST ABOVE THEIR RUMPUS.
THEIR WHAT?
BUTTOCKS. TUSH. CABOOSE. IT'S TRUE... SOMEONE MUST HAVE PASSED OUT A MEMO.
HOW DO YOU EVEN KNOW THIS?
WELL, IT CAN BE A LITTLE HARD TO OBSERVE, BUT IF THEY WEAR THEIR JEANS REAL LOW, YOU CAN JUST SEE—AW, HECK, I AM A SOCIAL SCIENTIST EXTRAORDINAIRE! I SHALL PROVE MY THEOREM EMPIRICALLY!!
NO NO NO NO NO NO NO NO NO NO
EXCUSE ME, MA'AM, BUT WOULD YOU MIND PULLING DOWN YOUR—
CRACK
...THE SCIENTIFIC LIFE IS FRAUGHT WITH PERIL.

This strip marked a transition for the character of the guard duck. Originally, he was just a violent and unpredictable duck. But here he became a delusional soldier who saw the rest of the world as a battlefield. I'm not sure what prompted the change, but it just seemed natural for the character. Believe it or not, I don't really think through these things. I just write what strikes me as funny, and if it seems to work, I write more of it. I know some people like to conceptualize characters and then write strips to fit that character. I like to just write strips and let the character form from that.

227

Since I'm always asked by readers to reveal what the crocs' accent is (the answer is that I don't have any specific accent in mind), I thought I'd have some fun by pretending to reveal it and then obliterating it with Liquid Paper.

This whole strip is based upon the climactic scene in the movie *Apocalypse Now*. Looking back on it, I now see that June was "movie reference month" in *Pearls*.

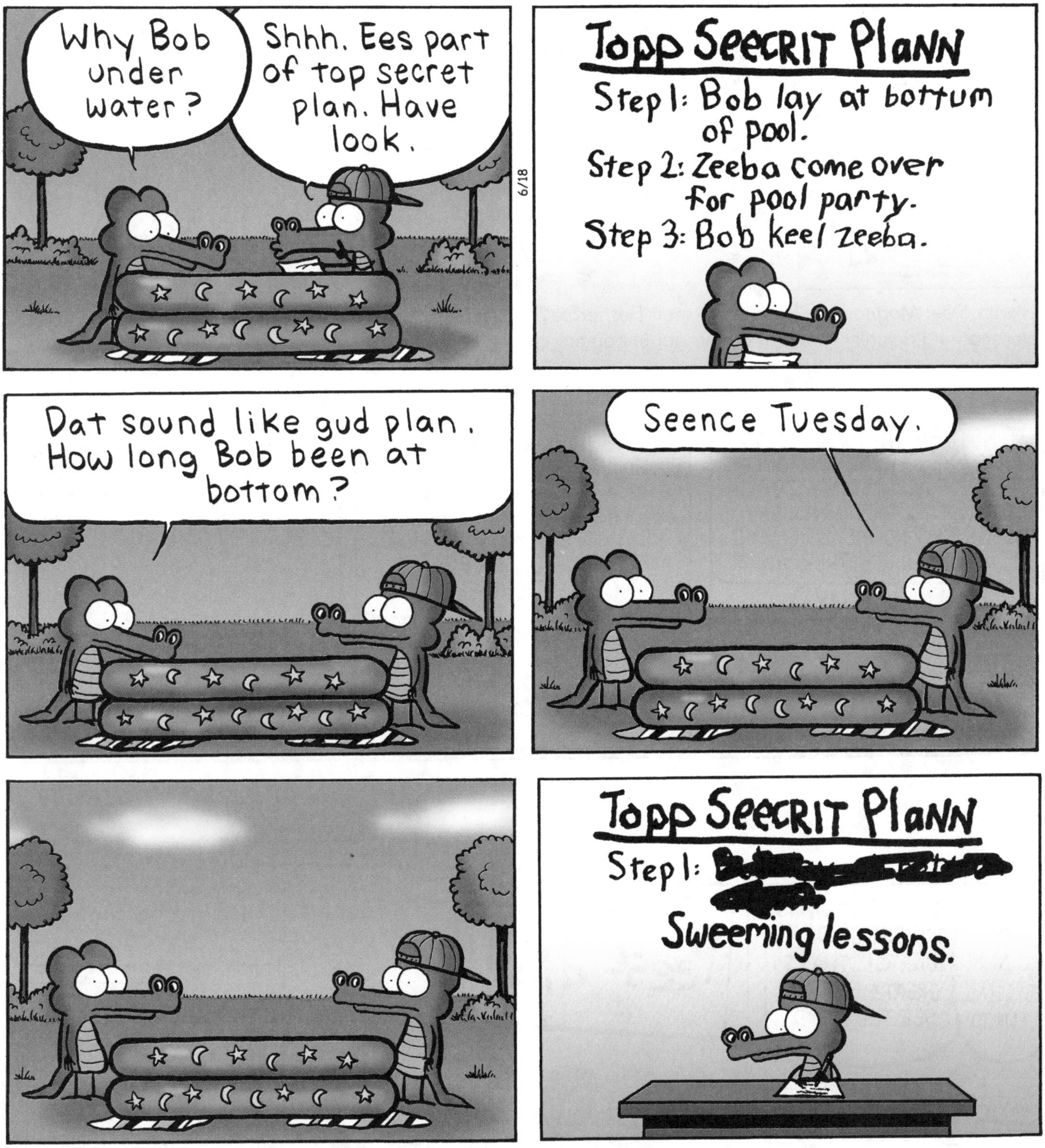
Why Bob under water?
Shhh. Ees part of top secret plan. Have look.
6/18
Topp Seecrit Plann
Step 1: Bob lay at bottum of pool.
Step 2: Zeeba come over for pool party.
Step 3: Bob keel zeeba.
Dat sound like gud plan. How long Bob been at bottom?
Seence Tuesday.
Topp Seecrit Plann
Step 1: [redacted]
Sweeming lessons.

As with *Steel Magnolias*, I have never seen *Desperate Housewives*. I could probably make better popular culture references if I actually knew something about popular culture.

Isn't it stupid how we always have to use these fake 555 telephone numbers like the one printed in the second panel here? It would be so much more satisfying to actually print one of my friends' phone numbers there and make his phone ring off the hook twenty-four hours a day.

I got the idea for this strip while staring at the lovebirds' cage at the San Francisco Zoo. The birds were chirping loudly at each other and the strip just sort of wrote itself.

I was really worried about this strip because it so clearly telegraphs a certain swear word (hint: it rhymes with "brass"). Thus, I ran it on a Saturday.

231

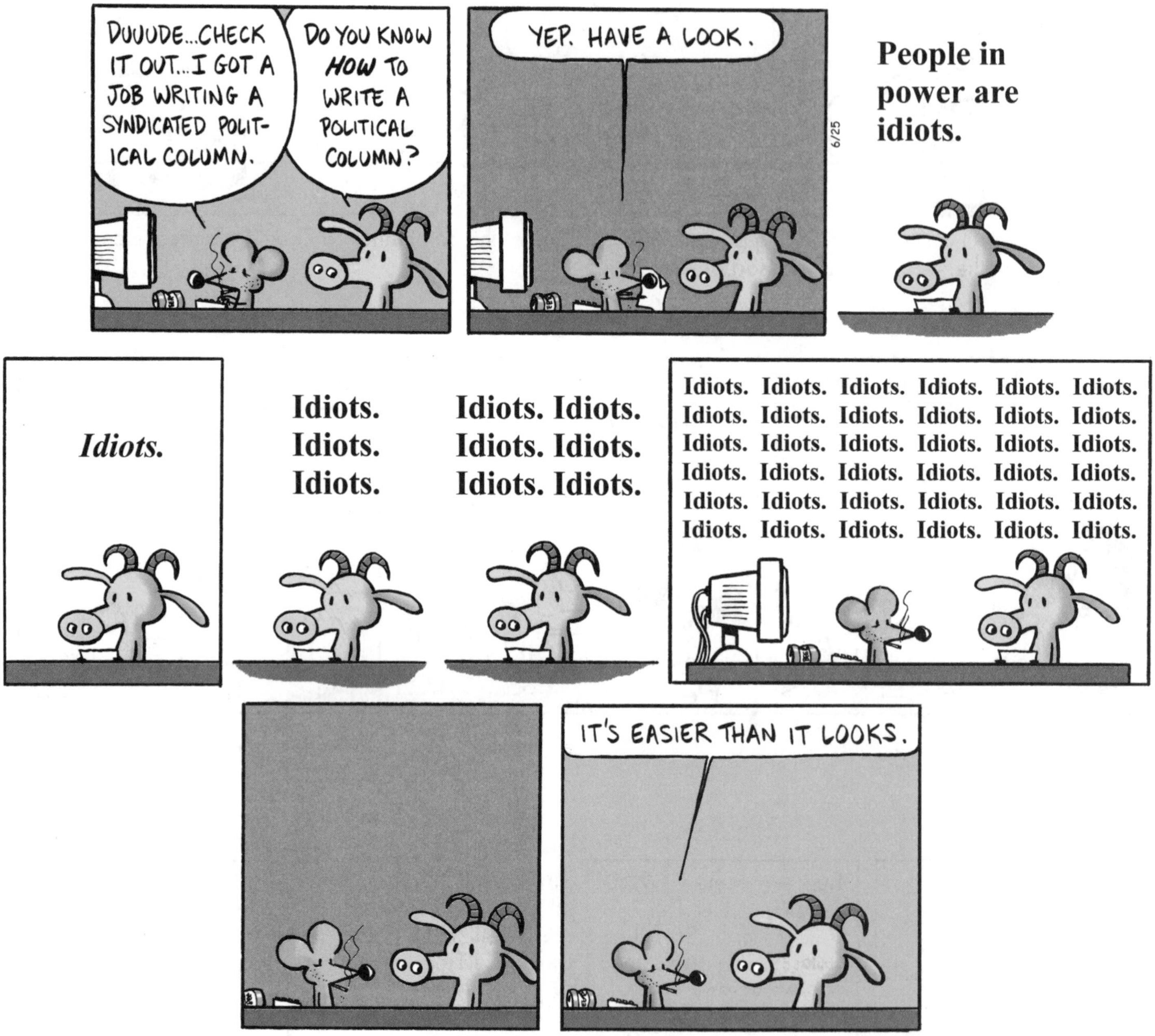
DUUUDE...CHECK IT OUT...I GOT A JOB WRITING A SYNDICATED POLITICAL COLUMN.
DO YOU KNOW HOW TO WRITE A POLITICAL COLUMN?
YEP. HAVE A LOOK.
6/25
People in power are idiots.
Idiots.
Idiots. Idiots. Idiots.
Idiots. Idiots. Idiots. Idiots. Idiots. Idiots.
Idiots. Idiots.
IT'S EASIER THAN IT LOOKS.

Shortly after doing this series, I heard from a woman in Newt Gingrich's office asking if Newt could have the original. I sent it to her, and in return I got a signed photo and book from Newt. Apparently, Newt liked the series but was a little confused by the symbolism of having his namesake killed by the crocodiles in the last strip. I told him not to worry because everyone dies in *Pearls*.

233

The dotted line around the speech balloon in the last panel indicates that the character is whispering. I have no idea why. It's just a comics rule, so I follow it.

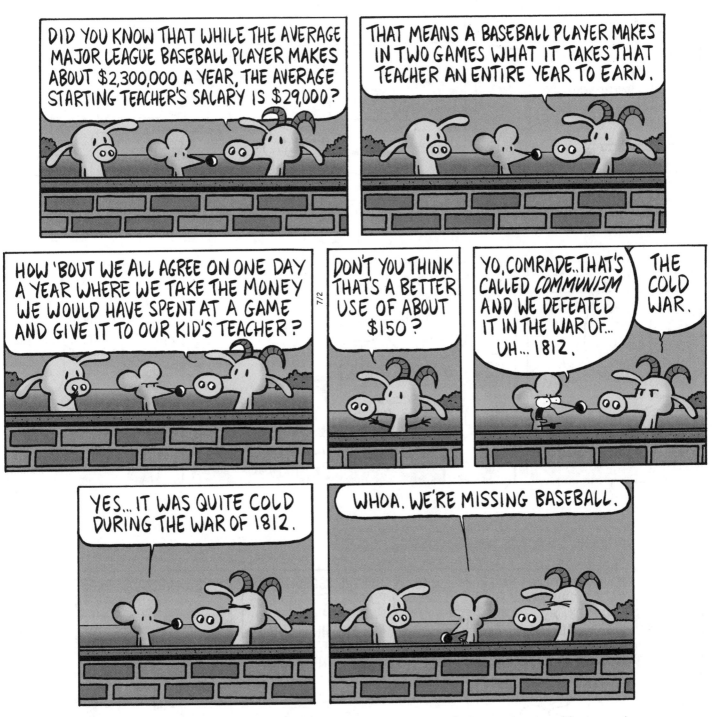

Goat really speaks for me here. I find it incredible how little we pay our kids' teachers and how much we pay our athletes. What does that say to our kids about the importance of their education?

I was talking to my cousin on the phone while I was inking this strip, and told him I would sneak the date of his birthday into the strip. So his birthday (6/10) appears on Pig's prison uniform.

While I often have Rat drinking beer in the strip, I almost always have Pig just drinking soda. Pig is like a little kid to me.

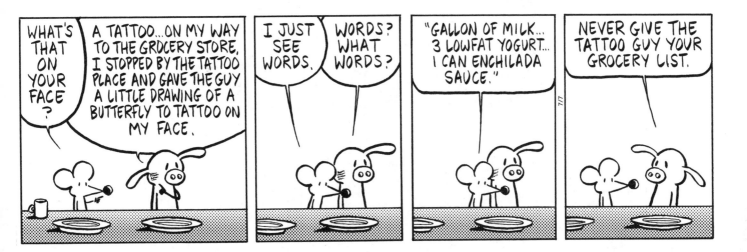

That zebra on the left is supposed to be wearing boxing gloves, although I see now that they look more like oven mitts. Oven mitts are not quite as threatening as boxing gloves.

Around the time of these duck strips, I was reading a great book about the Iraq War called *Generation Kill*. From it, I learned a lot of the terms and acronyms I use with the duck, such as "R.O.E." or "Rules of Engagement." Some of the most meaningful e-mails I get are the ones from soldiers serving in Iraq and Afghanistan. I was especially honored when one soldier told me that he went out on patrol with a picture of Rat taped to the windshield of his vehicle.

I used to write *Pearls* in my room at home, but now do most of the writing in a cafe near my house. Given the amount of time I spend there, I thought it only natural to try and give Rat a job at a cafe.

The first thing I did after I got the cafe job idea was to sit down with one of the employees at the cafe where I write the strip and ask him what the most annoying orders he gets are. He gave me the ones that appear in this strip and the next.

This hamper (which also appears in the previous Sunday strip) is the hamper that's in my bedroom at home. To draw it, I carried it downstairs and set it by my drawing table. That, my friends, is dedication.

240

I'm occasionally asked if I get paid by companies to mention their products. The answer is no. I've never even been approached.

Unlike the hamper, I did not pick up our garbage can from outside and put it by my drawing desk. I have my limits.

Whenever I hear Rat talking to his boss, I hear the voice of Ignatius J. Reilly in *A Confederacy of Dunces*. It's a great book, and if you haven't read it, you should.

The Vikings are very easy characters to write for. I just take something effeminate or artsy and have them involved with it. I think pretty much all comedy is about incongruity.

Of all the expressions I've ever drawn on Rat's face, I think this one might be my favorite.

The Vikings' line here came from the movie *Brokeback Mountain*. Or so I'm told. I've never actually seen it.

Too many words here. Holy smokes. I think this was a case of me really wanting to talk about the importance of campaign finance reform (an issue that I think lies at the heart of pretty much every other issue we have in this country), but a daily strip just wasn't the place to do it. It took much too long to set up and probably resulted in a number of people seeing all that dialogue and not even reading the strip that day.

243

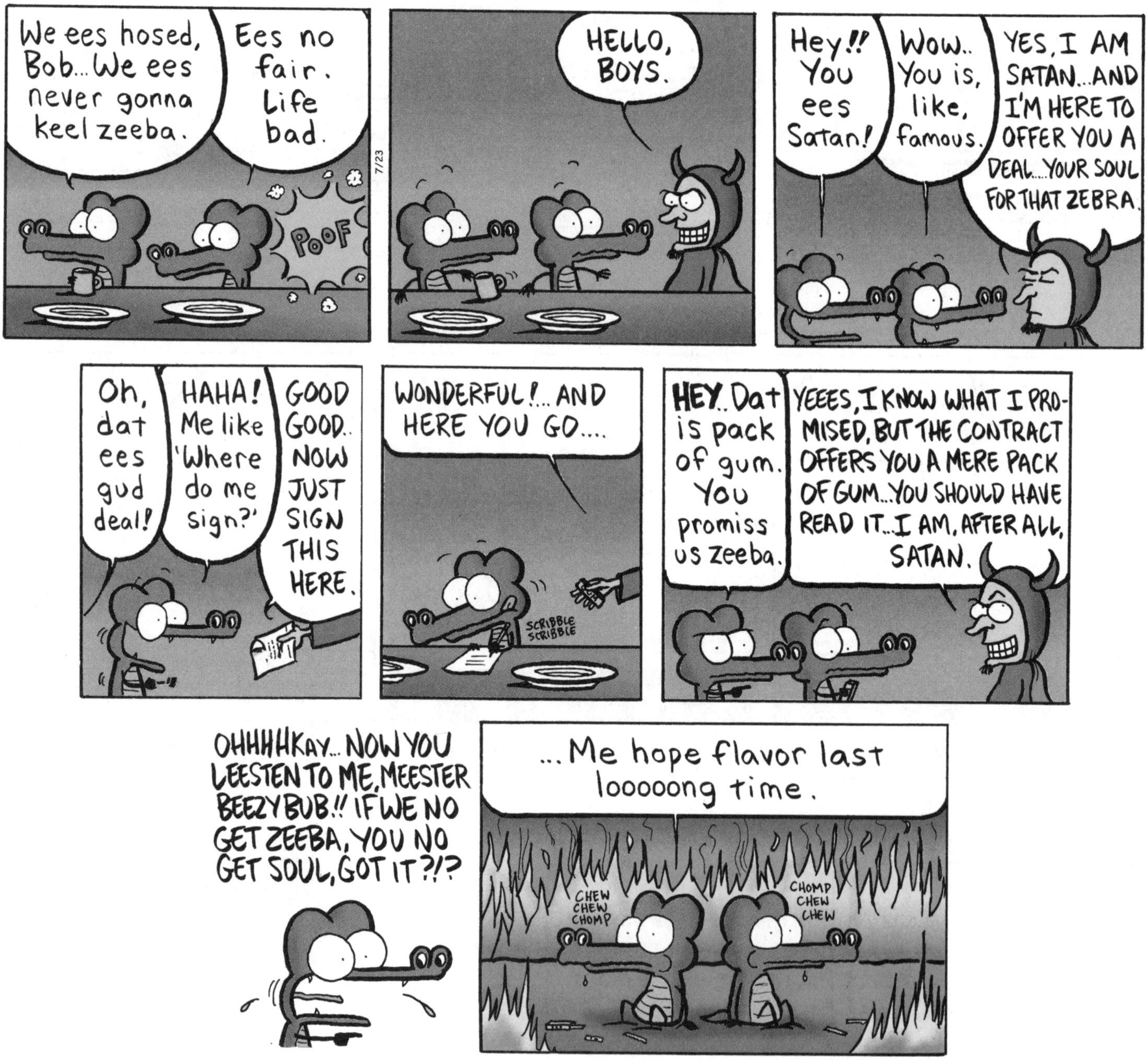
We ees hosed, Bob... We ees never gonna keel zeeba.
Ees no fair. Life bad.
7/23
POOF
HELLO, BOYS.
Hey!! You ees Satan!
Wow.. You is, like, famous.
YES, I AM SATAN... AND I'M HERE TO OFFER YOU A DEAL.... YOUR SOUL FOR THAT ZEBRA.
Oh, dat ees gud deal!
HAHA! Me like 'Where do me sign?'
GOOD GOOD.. NOW JUST SIGN THIS HERE.
WONDERFUL!... AND HERE YOU GO....
SCRIBBLE SCRIBBLE
HEY.. Dat is pack of gum. You promiss us zeeba.
YEEES, I KNOW WHAT I PROMISED, BUT THE CONTRACT OFFERS YOU A MERE PACK OF GUM... YOU SHOULD HAVE READ IT... I AM, AFTER ALL, SATAN.
OHHHHKAY... NOW YOU LEESTEN TO ME, MEESTER BEEZYBUB!! IF WE NO GET ZEEBA, YOU NO GET SOUL, GOT IT?!?
... Me hope flavor last looooong time.
CHEW CHEW CHOMP
CHOMP CHEW CHEW

I think every now and then it's a good idea to surprise readers with strips that don't match the normal tone of the comic. I think that's the case here with these two rain strips, both of which are a little more sad and touching than most *Pearls* strips. I believe that switching up tone every now and then helps keep the strip from becoming predictable.

One of the great things about cartoon characters is that you can change their body shape completely and then have them be normal again the next day. It gives you a lot of flexibility to write whatever you want. Of course, not every comic strip can do this. For example, if you did this sort of thing in a strip with a high level of reality like *For Better or For Worse*, it would look very out of place. That's why I don't write *For Better or For Worse*.

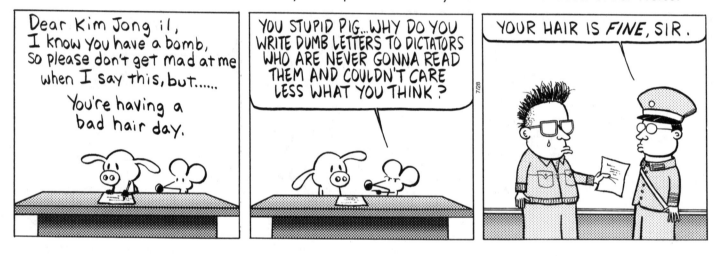

This whole strip is premised on the fact that these are pufferfish, which expand like this when they are threatened. But if you don't read the name on the mailbox in the first panel, you probably have no idea that they're pufferfish. I probably should have made that more prominent.

246

This generated complaints saying I was unfairly stereotyping all Middle Eastern men (a.k.a., "people with beards") as killers. The problem is that the line, "People with beards and some without beards and some in between try to kill you" just doesn't have the same impact.

I got this idea while staring out the cafe window at a poor little dog that was wearing one of these things.

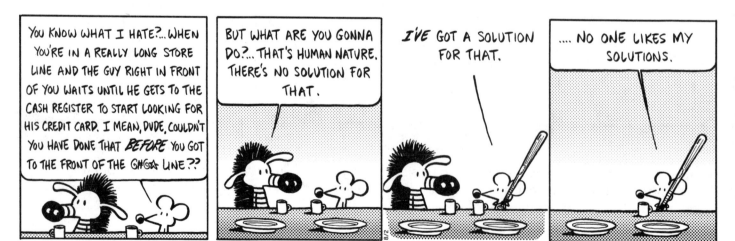

Rat's complaint is my complaint here. I give all my complaints to Rat.

I've heard of clubs like this, where the doorman checks you out to see if you look cool enough to get in. I can't believe people would actually stand in line to get rejected like that, especially when there are so many opportunities in life to get rejected *without* waiting.

This was a really old strip that I waited over two years to run because I didn't think it was very good. I'm not sure why I wait like that, though. Perhaps I think that like a fine wine, the joke will age to perfection.

Rat's line in the last panel reminds me of something I do when I drop my nine-year-old son off at school. After he gets out of the car and is about twenty yards away, I yell out to him, "And remember, don't hit anyone unless you really, really want to!" I just do it to see the look on the other parents' faces. And on that note of sound advice, I say goodbye 'til the next treasury.

The Not Ready for Prime Time Comic Strips

Twenty of the twenty-one strips in this section were either pulled prior to publication or significantly edited. Most were pulled or edited because the subject matter was likely to cause problems, i.e., complaints, confusion, letters to the editor, etc. Some were pulled because I thought they were just plain bad. The last of these twenty-one strips is simply a comic that I was not able to finish because I could not think up an ending.

Thanks
for
listening.

This strip and the next five that follow were originally set to run immediately after the January 23, 2005, Sunday strip where Rat's head exploded (the last published strip in *Lions and Tigers and Crocs, Oh My!*). But the premise was so confusing and involved (as you can see from the sheer number of words in this strip) that I finally just gave up on the whole thing and nixed the entire week. It killed me to lose six strips, and I'm still not entirely sure it was the right decision, but I did it. So here is the series, for the first time in print.

This strip sort of worried me as well, given that I am dependent on these newspaper people for my living.

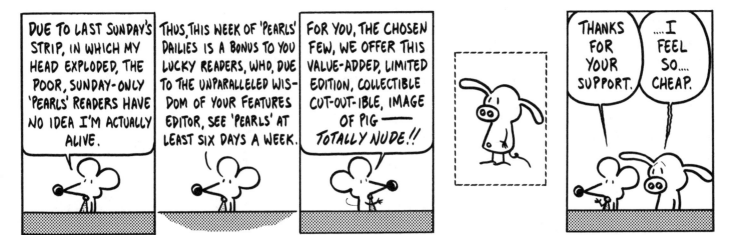

255

OVER THE PAST WEEK, SOME 'PEARLS' READERS HAVE CROWED THAT NONE OF THE NEWSPAPER LIMITATIONS REGARDING THE DISTINCTION BETWEEN DAILY-ONLY AND SUNDAY-ONLY READERS APPLY TO THEM.

THIS IS BECAUSE THEY READ ALL THE DAILY AND SUNDAY 'PEARLS' STRIPS ON THE INTERNET.

WHILE THIS MAY BE TRUE, IT IS HARDLY FAIR. THUS, CONSCIOUS OF THE LIMITATIONS OF COMPUTER MONITOR RESOLUTION AND MINDFUL OF THE NEED TO BALANCE THE SCALES, WE OFFER THIS—THE SECRET OF LIFE—VIEWABLE TO ANY NEWSPAPER READER WITH A GOOD EYE, BUT INDISCERNABLE TO INTERNET READERS.

THE SECRET O'LIFE!

beer

Pearls
keeping newspapers relevant for over two years

CHEERS.

AS PART OF THIS WEEK'S BONUS STRIPS, WE HERE AT 'PEARLS' OFFER YOU LUCKY READERS THIS FUN PUZZLE... SIMPLY FIND THE SEVEN DIFFERENCES BETWEEN THE NEXT TWO PANELS.

HOW'D YOU DO?

ANSWERS:
1) Milk levitating over characters' heads; 2) Pencil levitating over characters' heads; 3) Orange levitating over characters' heads; 4) Toilet paper levitating over characters' heads; 5) Cube of butter levitating over characters' heads; 6) Banana levitating over characters' heads; 7) Oh, c'mon, you didn't think I'd give you ALL the answers, did you?

This was my favorite strip in this otherwise ill-fated series.

IN THIS, THE FINAL STRIP OF THIS WEEK'S BONUS DAILIES, WE'D LIKE TO RESPOND TO THE MANY REQUESTS WE'VE GOTTEN HERE AT PEARLS, INC. FOR A HOW-TO GUIDE TO DRAWING PIG... JUST FOLLOW THESE EASY STEPS AND YOU, TOO, CAN BE YOUR VERY OWN STEPHAN PASTIS...ENJOY!

STEP 1: DRAW A SMALL OVAL IN THE CENTER OF THE PAGE...THIS WILL BE PIG'S NOSE.

STEP 2: FILL IN THE REST!

JOIN US TOMORROW FOR THE TRIUMPHAL UNDEATH OF ME!

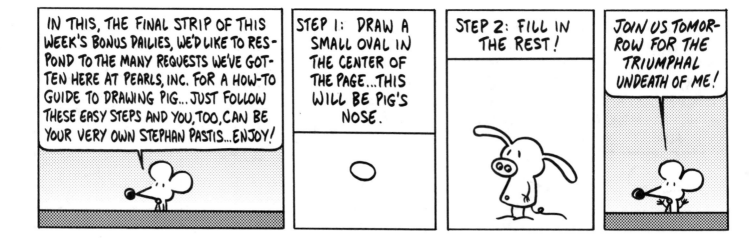

256

This was the original of the January 30, 2005, Sunday strip that appears on page 13 of this book. It had to be changed for the same reason the *Cathy* Sunday strips at the end of *Lions and Tigers and Crocs, Oh My!* had to be changed, which was that there were a number of prominent hostage beheadings going on in Iraq at the time.

I did this strip shortly after the whole Mel Gibson fiasco happened (where he allegedly said a bunch of this stuff to some police officers who pulled him over). Because it was a news item that everyone knew about, I thought it was safe to make fun of it in the comics. But it clearly gave my syndicate pause. They didn't tell me that I *couldn't* do it, but they let me know it could cause real problems. So I pulled it at the last minute.

This is the original of the February 21, 2005, strip mentioned earlier in the book.

This one was just so weak I couldn't run it. And I have pretty low standards. So that's saying something.

This series of four strips had every malady imaginable. It was bizarre. It didn't make sense. It used the word "hootchie." And it touched upon racial issues. Why I drew it, I'll never know. But here it is.

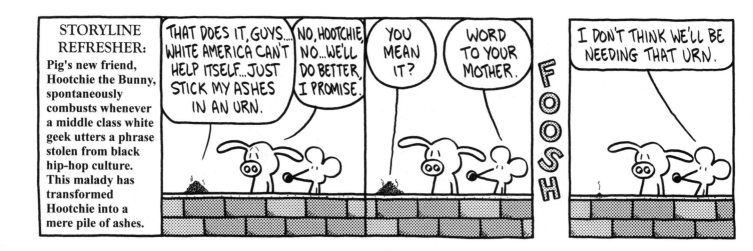

This is the nixed tree strip that I mentioned earlier in the book. As stated, it is the only one of the three tree strips that I pulled from publication, and I did it just because I thought it was too weak to publish. That of course doesn't stop me from putting it in this book.

This was the original of the June 16, 2005, strip that appears on page 72 of this book. I'm not sure why I decided to change it. Looking back on it, I think this original was probably funnier than the modified version.

This is the original version of the "No Repro" Sunday strip. The final panel has the quote from the movie *Cool Hand Luke* instead of the *Terminator 2* quote you saw earlier in the book.

This one's strange. And bad. Please, don't look.

This is the realtor strip discussed on page 141 of this book. Again, I just thought it was too unfair to run. Also, for what it's worth, I originally included my editor's name with the syndicate's address in that last panel, so that all the complaints would go directly to him. He thought that was a bit too much and asked that I delete it. Still, I was surprised that they let me include their address at all.

This is the original of the April 20, 2006, strip mentioned earlier in the book.

This is an odd one. It's a Sunday strip I started drawing without having any ending in mind. As a cartoonist, you really shouldn't do this because you risk doing the work and then not being able to finish it. Well, that's what happened here. I just got stuck and couldn't figure out a decent ending. Thus, I present, The Unfinished Comic Strip.